What Readers Are Saying About *Grails: A Quick-Start Guide*

This book, like Grails, is common sense distilled. You'll be productive in Grails in no time.

▶ **Scott Davis**
Founder, ThirstyHead.com

This book stands heads and shoulders above other Groovy and Grails books available today. Dave's practical, hands-on approach will teach you the nuts and bolts of the language and framework and then lead you through a project, step-by-step. This mix of instruction and practice is the perfect introduction to both Groovy and Grails.

▶ **Jared Richardson**
Consultant, Agile Artisans.com

The Grails web framework is all about productivity, and so is *Grails: A Quick-Start Guide*. Dave Klein builds a serious application throughout the chapters, as if you were working with a colleague teaching you new technology. This guide will get you productive in hours, not weeks, and thanks to Dave's humor, you're really going to enjoy learning Grails. If you need to dive into Grails for your next project, this book is for you!

▶ **Guillaume Laforge**
Groovy project manager, SpringSource

Dave Klein's book is an enjoyable read that presents an efficient path to get from Grails novice to productive programmer. Anyone developing a web application to run on a JVM should read this book.

▶ **Steven Harris**
Director of engineering, Terracotta

This book was an excellent guide for me as a first-time user of Grails as well as Groovy. Building an entire project while learning is a big asset: it is one thing to read and learn; it is another to learn by example. The book presents the subject matter creatively and simplifies it. It is definitely a recommended guide to those beginners who are ready to take on a challenge with Grails and Groovy.

▶ **Amer Ghumrawi**
Programmer/analyst, WinWholesale, Inc.

I've always believed that a good programmer finds the information they need when they need it. Nothing could be more true to that statement than with this book. I am new to Grails development and was looking for a good book/reference guide. I found it in *Grails: A Quick-Start Guide*. Even after reading it, I found myself referring to it often to help me along. It was not written at a level that assumes the reader is an expert Java developer or familiar with the popular frameworks. I found it easy to understand, and the code examples were excellent in displaying the ease with which a relative newcomer can become a Groovy developer using Grails. I highly recommend this book for anyone who is just starting to develop Grails applications.

▶ **Doug Burns**
Programmer/analyst

I've read several books on the Grails framework, and this is the first that explained things enough that I felt confident building something from scratch. If you know Ruby on Rails, you should definitely look at this framework, and this book really helps you get your feet wet.

▶ **Brian Hogan**
Rails consultant and trainer

Great book! Dave does a fantastic job of presenting the framework in an easy-to-follow and very accessible way. Excellent!

▶ **Jeff Brown**
Core Grails developer

Grails
A Quick-Start Guide

Grails
A Quick-Start Guide

Dave Klein

The Pragmatic Bookshelf
Raleigh, North Carolina   Dallas, Texas

Our Pragmatic courses, workshops, and other products can help you and your team create better software and have more fun. For more information, as well as the latest Pragmatic titles, please visit us at

http://www.pragprog.com

Printed in the United States of America.

ISBN-10: 1-934356-46-8
ISBN-13: 978-1-934356-46-3
Printed on acid-free paper.
P1.0 printing, October 2009
Version: 2009-9-30

Contents

Chapter 1

Introduction

1.1 Let Me Tell You About Grails. . .

Web development is a very rewarding experience. Building an application that can run from anywhere in the world is pretty awesome. Even in a corporate environment, you can deliver new features to your users, no matter where they are located, without ever touching their computer. It's a beautiful thing. Consider also what you can build: the potential for creativity on the Web is unlimited.

The Java platform brings even more power to the party. The Java Servlet API and the plethora of libraries and frameworks in the Java ecosystem make it possible to include almost any feature you could want in a web application. It is an exciting time to be a web developer. However, it's not all sweetness and light.

With all this power comes a level of complexity that can be daunting. With most Java-based web frameworks, there are multiple XML configuration files to deal with, along with classes to extend and interfaces to implement. As a project grows, this complexity seems to increase exponentially.

Many web application frameworks have been created to address this problem. So many Java web frameworks have been developed that you might ask, "Why Grails? Why another framework?" That was my thought when I first heard about Grails.

I was at a conference that featured sessions on an array of Java-related technologies and was planning to attend several talks on JavaServer Faces (JSF), which is what I was working with at the time. During one of the time slots where there was nothing JSF-related, I wandered into a session on Grails by Scott Davis. And I have to say, I was impressed. But not convinced.

In the past, I had worked with so-called rapid application development tools on the desktop and had seen the trade-off that you had to make to get these "applications in minutes." As soon as you needed to do more than the tool was designed for, you were stuck. I didn't want to go down that road again. Still, Grails did look like it would be a good choice for *small* applications. So, I gave it a try.

After using Grails to build a website for our local Java user group, I was hooked. By day, I was struggling with JSF and Enterprise JavaBeans (EJB); by night, I was having a blast building a website with Grails. I began to look for ways to take advantage of the brilliant simplicity of Grails in my day job. After all, I worked in a Java shop, and Grails is a fully compliant JEE[1] framework. It would produce a standard .war file, which could be deployed on our commercial JEE application server. Finally, an opportunity presented itself.

It was a small but important public-facing web application, planned as a six-week JSF/EJB project. With Grails, it was done in three weeks—and it turned out to be a little less trivial than we thought, because we needed to integrate with an existing EJB server. We found that the Grails "magic" was great for most of the application and provided significant productivity boosts. We also found that when we needed to do something Grails didn't handle "out of the box,"[2] it was easy to dip into the underlying technologies and do what we needed. There were no black boxes or brick walls. It wasn't "the Grails way or the highway."

We went on to use Grails to rescue another, much larger project that was in trouble, with similar results. Grails is definitely not *just* for small applications!

1.2 How Does Grails Do It?

Grails takes a set of successful frameworks, each of which has made its own strides toward addressing the complexity of building web applications, and makes them all simpler, easier to use, and ultimately more powerful.

---

1. Java Enterprise Edition.
2. I use this term with some hesitation—see http://dave-klein.blogspot.com/2008/08/out-of-box.html.

Grails bundles Spring, Hibernate, Sitemesh, HSQLDB, Jetty, and a host of other battle-hardened frameworks, and following the principle of "convention over configuration,"[3] it removes the complexity for most use cases. And it uses the dynamic Groovy programming language to magically give us easy access to the combined power of these tools.

Recall from my story that on the projects I was involved in, Grails was a replacement for both JSF and EJB. JSF, like Struts before it and JSP before that, is intended to address the web tier (the front end). EJB was the framework we were using to provide persistence, transactions, and various other services (the back end). Grails addresses the whole application, and more important, it allows *us* to address the whole application. Using the frameworks mentioned earlier, Grails gives us a complete, seamless MVC[4] framework that is really more of a web application platform than just another framework.

1.3 Why This Book?

The idea for this book came about while working on the projects I mentioned earlier. I had been working with Grails for a while, but four other developers were working with me, and we really could have used a book to help bring them up to speed quickly. They didn't need a reference book yet but something more than a collection of articles and blog posts (as helpful as those are).

As Grails' exposure and acceptance continues to grow and as more and more developers have their "wow!" moments, it will become even more important to have a resource to help them get started quickly. That's the goal of this quick-start guide. It is not intended to be a reference or the only Grails book on your shelf. In this book, I'll help you get started and become productive with Grails, but you will no doubt want to go beyond that. To help you dig deeper, I've included lists of books, websites, blogs, and other helpful resources from the Groovy/Grails community in Appendix B, on page 203.

This book is, however, intended to be more than a cursory introduction. We will cover all the basics of Grails and a few advanced topics as well. When we have finished our time together here, you will understand Grails well enough to use it in real projects. In fact, you will have

---

3. See http://en.wikipedia.org/wiki/Convention_over_Configuration.
4. Model View Controller. See http://en.wikipedia.org/wiki/Model-view-controller.

already used it in a real project, because that is what we are going to do together. More on that later.

1.4 Who Should Read This Book

This book is aimed at web developers looking for relief from the pain brought on by the complexity of modern web development. If you dream in XML and enjoy juggling multiple layers of abstraction at a time or if you are in a job where your pay is based on the number of lines of code you write, then Grails may not be for you. If, on the other hand, you are looking for a way to be more productive, a way to be able to focus on the heart of your applications instead of all the technological bureaucracy, then you're in the right place.

I am assuming an understanding of web application development, but you don't need to be an expert to benefit from Grails and from this book. An understanding of Java or another object-oriented programming language would be helpful. If you have experience with Spring and Hibernate, you are ahead of the curve, but if you've never even heard of them, you'll do fine. You can go quite far with Grails and be using Spring and Hibernate extensively without even realizing it. Finally, the language of Grails is Groovy. I won't assume that you have any experience with Groovy, and you won't need a great deal of it to get going with Grails. However, some knowledge of Groovy syntax and constructs will be helpful, so we'll now embark on a brief tutorial.

1.5 Source Code

The code for the project in this book is available for download. You can find a link to the source code on the book's home page: http://pragprog. com/titles/dkgrails. At the top of most code listings, there is a gray box that shows where this code can be found in the source code repository. In the PDF version of the book, this is a link directly to the code file. You'll notice that the path shown in these boxes is different from the one suggested in the text; this is because we have multiple snapshots of the project at different stages, one for each chapter.

Grails Versions

The examples in this book have been tested with Grails 1.1.1. Grails 1.2 is in the works and will be bringing several new features. Keep an eye on the *Grails: A Quick-Start Guide* blog (http://gquick.blogspot.com) for any potential breaking changes and workarounds.

1.6 Enough Groovy to Be Dangerous

Groovy is a dynamic language for the Java Virtual Machine (JVM). Of all the JVM languages, Groovy has the best integration with Java and probably the lowest barrier to entry for Java developers. Java is considered by many to be in the "C family" of languages; that is to say that its syntax borrows heavily from the C language. Other languages in this family are C++, C#, and, by its close relationship to Java, Groovy. Without getting into a debate on whether that syntax family is a good one, it is one that millions of developers are familiar with. That means that millions of developers can quickly pick up Groovy!

Groovy—like Spring, Hibernate, and the other frameworks used in Grails—is included in the Grails install. You do not need to install Groovy to use Grails. However, Groovy is a great multipurpose language, and I encourage you to download it and take it for a spin. You will quickly become more productive in areas like XML processing, database access, file manipulation, and more. You can download the Groovy installation and find more information on the Groovy website.[5] Some excellent books are available on Groovy such as Venkat Subramaniam's *Programming Groovy* [Sub08], Scott Davis's *Groovy Recipes: Greasing the Wheels of Java* [Dav08], and *Groovy in Action* [Koe07] by Dierk König and friends.

We're going to discuss the Groovy features that are most often used in a Grails application. But first, for the benefit of Java developers, we'll look at some of the differences between Java and Groovy.

1.7 Groovy Syntax Compared to Java

Despite the overall syntactic similarities, there are some differences between Groovy and Java that are worth noting. The first thing you'll notice in a block of Groovy code is the lack of semicolons; in Groovy, semicolons are optional. Return statements are also optional. If there is no return statement in a method, then the last statement evaluated is returned. Sometimes this makes sense, especially in the case of small

---

5. http://groovy.codehaus.org

methods that simply return a value or perform a single calculation. Other times it can be confusing. That's the beauty of the word *optional*. When **return** makes code more readable, use it; when it doesn't, don't.

Parentheses for method calls are optional in most cases, the exception being when calling a method without any arguments. Here are some examples:

```
x = someMethodWithArgs arg1, arg2, arg3
y = someMethodWithoutArgs()
```

Methods without arguments need the parentheses so that Groovy can tell them apart from *properties*. Groovy provides "real" properties.[6] All fields in a Groovy class are given *getters* and *setters* at compile time. When you access a field of a Groovy class, it may look like you are directly accessing the field, but behind the scenes, the getter or setter is being called. If you're not convinced, you can call them explicitly. They'll be there even though you didn't code them.

introduction/get_property.groovy

```
class Person {
    String name
}
def person = new Person()
person.name = 'Abigail'
assert person.getName() == 'Abigail'
person.setName('Abi')
assert person.name == 'Abi'
```

If you *explicitly declare* a get or set method for a property, it will be used as expected.

introduction/explicit_set_property.groovy

```
class Person {
    String name

    void setName(String val){
        name = val.toUpperCase()
    }
}

def person = new Person(name:'Sarah')
assert person.name == 'SARAH'
```

---

6. Joe Nuxoll provides a good explanation of the concept of properties at http://blogs.sun.com/joe/resource/java-properties-events.pdf.

The previous snippet shows a few other differences in Groovy. First, all Groovy classes automatically get a named-args constructor. This is a constructor that takes a Map and calls the set method for each key that corresponds to a property.[7] You can easily see how this might save several lines of code with larger classes. Grails takes advantage of this feature to assign the values from a web page to a new object instance. Second, in Groovy, types are optional. Instead of giving a variable an explicit type, we can use the **def** keyword to designate that this variable will be *dynamically* typed. The third difference is the use of == in the assert statements. In Groovy, == is the same as calling the equals() method on the left operand.

Now, the toUpperCase() method we just used is the same as in Java. But for a little fun, we can modify that last example to try one of the many methods that Groovy adds to the String class.[8]

`introduction/reverse.groovy`

```
class Person {
    String name

    void setName(String val){
        name = val.toUpperCase().reverse()
    }
}

Person p = new Person(name:'Hannah')

assert p.name == 'HANNAH'
```

It worked. Trust me.

Not only does Groovy enhance the java.lang.String class, but it also adds an entirely new one.

1.8 Groovy Strings

Groovy adds a new string known as a GString. A GString can be created by declaring a literal with double quotes; a string literal with single quotes is a java.lang.String. A GString can be used in place of a Java String. If

---

7. Any elements in the map that do not correspond to a property are ignored by the named-args constructor.
8. You can find more goodies in the API docs at http://groovy.codehaus.org/groovy-jdk/java/lang/String.html.

a method is expecting a String and is given a GString, it will be cast at runtime.

The beauty and power of the GString is its ability to evaluate embedded Groovy expressions. Groovy expressions can be designated in two ways. For simple values that are not directly adjacent to any plain text, you can just use a dollar sign, like this:

```
"Hello $name"
```

For more involved expressions, you can use the dollar sign and a pair of curly braces:

```
"The 5th letter in 'Encyclopedia' is ${'Encyclopedia'[4]}"
```

There can be any number of expressions in a given GString, and single quotes can be embedded without any escaping. This comes in handy when generating HTML, as we'll see later. For now, let's take a look at the GString in action.

introduction/hello_groovy_string.groovy

```
def name = 'Zachary'
def x = 3
def y = 7
def groovyString = "Hello ${name}, did you know that $x x $y equals ${x*y}?"

assert groovyString == 'Hello Zachary, did you know that 3 x 7 equals 21?'
```

1.9 Groovy Closures

A Groovy closure, in simple terms, is an executable block of code that can be assigned to a variable, passed to a method, and executed.[9] Many of the enhancements Groovy has made to the standard Java libraries involved adding methods that take a closure as a parameter.

A closure is declared by placing code between curly braces. It can be declared as it is being passed to a method call, or it can be assigned to a variable and used later. A closure can take parameters by listing them after the opening curly brace and separating them from the code with a *dash-rocket* (->), like so:

```
def c = {a, b ->  a + b}
```

---

9. There has been much discussion and some confusion over the definition of a "closure" in programming languages. Some argue that what Groovy defines as a closure isn't. If you're ever in town, we can discuss it over a cup of coffee, but for our purposes, we'll be referring to closures as defined at http://groovy.codehaus.org/Closures.

If no parameters are declared in a closure, then one is implicitly provided: it's called it. Take a look at the following example:

introduction/closure_times.groovy

```
def name = 'Dave'
def c = {println "$name called this closure ${it+1} time${it > 0 ? 's' : ''}"}
assert c instanceof Closure
5.times(c)
```

There's a fair bit of new stuff in these three lines of code. Let's start at the top. The variable name is available when the closure is executed. Anything that is in scope when the closure is created will be available when it is executed, even if it is being executed by code in a different class. The closure is being assigned to the variable c and has no declared parameters. It does have and use the implicit parameter it. The code in this closure takes advantage of another Groovy shortcut. What would be in Java System.out.println() is now just println(). When you look at the text of the GString that follows, it becomes obvious that this code will work only if whatever calls this closure passes it a single parameter that is a number. That's just what the times() method, which Groovy adds to Integer, does. The parentheses are not required for the times() method, but I added them to emphasize that the closure was being passed in as a parameter. The output from this code looks like this:

```
Dave called this Closure 1 time
Dave called this Closure 2 times
Dave called this Closure 3 times
Dave called this Closure 4 times
Dave called this Closure 5 times
```

There is much more to the Groovy closure than we can cover here, and I highly recommend the coverage of this topic in *Programming Groovy* [Sub08]. We will see more examples of Closures in action as we look at Groovy collection classes.

1.10 Groovy Collections

Groovy offers many enhancements to the standard Java collection classes. We'll take a look at the three collection types that are most used in Grails. The List, Map, and Set are powerful tools, and Groovy gives them a new edge. I know—technically Map is not a Collection; that is, it does not implement the Collection interface. But for our purposes, it is a *collection* in that it holds objects. So, leaving semantic sensitivities aside, let's look at what Groovy has done for these classes.

List

One of the first interesting things to learn about the List in Groovy is that it can be created with a literal declaration.

introduction/groovy_list.groovy

```groovy
def colors = ['Red', 'Green', 'Blue', 'Yellow']
def empty = []

assert colors instanceof List
assert empty instanceof List
assert empty.class.name == 'java.util.ArrayList'
```

A comma-separated list inside square brackets is an initialized List. It can contain literal numbers, strings, or any other objects. This is a good time to point out that in Groovy *everything* is an object. Even simple data types such as int or boolean are autoboxed objects. (That's why we were able to call the times() method on the literal 5 in our earlier example.) The last line of this example shows that the default List implementation in Groovy is a java.util.ArrayList.

Groovy has also added a host of helpful methods to the List interface. One of the most useful is each(). This method is actually added to all objects in Groovy, but it is most useful with collection types. The each() method on List takes a closure as a parameter and calls that closure for each element in the List, passing in that element as the single "it" parameter.

introduction/groovy_list.groovy

```groovy
def names = ['Nate', 'Matthew', 'Craig', 'Amanda']

names.each{
  println "The name $it contains ${it.size()} characters."
}
```

This example will print the following output to the console:

```
The name Nate contains 4 characters.
The name Matthew contains 7 characters.
The name Craig contains 5 characters.
The name Amanda contains 6 characters.
```

Two handy methods added by Groovy are min() and max():

introduction/groovy_list.groovy

```groovy
assert names.min() == 'Amanda'
assert names.max() == 'Nate'
```

Groovy also provides a few easy ways to sort a List. The simple sort() will provide a natural sort of the elements in the List. The sort() method can also take a closure. If the closure has no explicit parameters, then the implied it parameter can be used in an expression to sort on. You can also give the closure two parameters to represent two List elements and then use those parameters in a comparison expression. Here are some examples:

introduction/groovy_list.groovy

```groovy
def sortedNames = names.sort()
assert sortedNames == ['Amanda','Craig','Matthew','Nate']

sortedNames = names.sort{it.size()}
assert sortedNames == ['Nate','Craig','Amanda','Matthew']

sortedNames = names.sort{obj1, obj2 ->
  obj1[2] <=> obj2[2]
}
assert sortedNames == ['Craig','Amanda','Nate','Matthew']
```

The first example performs a natural sort on the names. The second example uses a closure to sort the names based on their size(). The last example, though admittedly contrived, is the more interesting one. In that example, we pass a closure to the sort(). This closure takes two parameters that represent two objects to be compared. In the body of the closure, we use the comparison operator[10] to compare some aspect of the two objects; in this case, and this is the contrived part, we compare the third character in the name with [2]. This type of sort would make more sense when the List elements are a more complex type and you need to sort on a combination of properties or a more complex expression—but you get the point.

Another useful feature of List is that the left shift operator (<<) can be used in place of the add() method:

introduction/groovy_list.groovy

```groovy
names << 'Jim'
assert names.contains('Jim')
```

---

10. <=> is a shortcut for the compareTo() method.

Map

The Map class contains a collection of key/value pairs. It also can be created with a literal declaration, like so:

introduction/groovy_map.groovy

```
def family = [boys:7, girls:6, Debbie:1, Dave:1]
def empty = [:]

assert family instanceof Map
assert empty instanceof Map
assert empty.getClass().name == 'java.util.LinkedHashMap'
```

The Map class in Groovy also has the each() method. When it is given a closure without any parameters, the implicit it will be a Map.Entry containing key and value properties. The more common approach is to give the closure two parameters. The first parameter will hold the key, and the second parameter will hold the value.

introduction/groovy_map.groovy

```
def favoriteColors = [Ben:'Green',Solomon:'Blue',Joanna:'Red']
favoriteColors.each{key, value ->
    println "${key}'s favorite color is ${value}."
}
```

The output from this code would be as follows:

```
Ben's favorite color is Green.
Solomon's favorite color is Blue.
Joanna's favorite color is Red.
```

In Groovy, Map entries can be accessed using dot notation, as if they were properties. You may have noticed that in our first Map example, we had to use empty.getClass().name instead of the Groovy shortcut empty.class.name. That's because empty.class would have looked for a key in empty called class. Other than a few edge cases like that, this is the preferred way to access Map values.

introduction/groovy_map.groovy

```
assert favoriteColors.Joanna == 'Red'
```

There is no overridden left shift operator for Map, but adding an element is still a snap. Assigning a value to a key that doesn't exist will add that key and value to the Map.

introduction/groovy_map.groovy

```
favoriteColors.Rebekah = 'Pink'
assert favoriteColors.size() == 4
assert favoriteColors.containsKey('Rebekah')
```

Set

The Set class also implements the Collection interface, so most of what we saw with List applies to it as well. Set is the default type for one-to-many associations in Grails, so we'll be working with it often. There are a couple of notable differences between Set and List. First, a Set can't contain duplicates, and second, it can't be accessed with the subscript operator ([]). This last difference can be a hindrance, but it is easy to overcome with the toList() method.

```
introduction/groovy_set.groovy
```

```groovy
def employees = ['Susannah','Noah','Samuel','Gideon'] as Set
Set empty = []

assert employees instanceof Set
assert empty instanceof Set
assert empty.class.name == 'java.util.HashSet'

employees << 'Joshua'

assert employees.contains('Joshua')

println employees.toList()[4]
```

In this example, we create a Set with four names in it. Since we didn't declare employees with a type, we need to cast it as a Set. (The default type for a literal declaration like this is ArrayList.) We could have just declared the type explicitly, as we do with empty on the next line. Then we add another item to the Set using the handy left shift operator and assert() that it is there. Finally, we show that there are now five items by printing the fifth one with println employees.toList()[4]. This is the output from the last line of that example: Samuel. This brings up another point about Set: you have no control of the order in which elements are stored. If you need to specify an order, either sorted or creation order, you can use a SortedSet or List.

Many more methods are added to these classes that we don't have space to cover here. To become more productive in Groovy (and to have more "wow!" moments), check out the Groovy JDK docs at http://groovy.codehaus.org/groovy-jdk.

1.11 Where to from Here?

Now that you have some Groovy basics under your belt, we are ready to get into Grails. Over the next 11 chapters, we will be exploring most areas of the Grails framework. We won't spend a great deal of time on any one feature, and we may not cover every aspect of Grails. The goal is to give you the knowledge and experience necessary to start working effectively and productively with Grails and to point you to the resources you'll need as you continue.

"Experience?" you say. "How do I get experience from a book?" This book is meant not only to be read but to be *used*. In the Groovy tutorial, I showed some code snippets and explained them. In the rest of the book, we will be working together on a real project. By the time you finish this book, you will have developed and deployed your first full-featured web application with Grails.

Finally, at the end of the book, there is an appendix containing resources (websites, blogs, mailing lists) available in the thriving Groovy and Grails community.

Let's get started.

1.12 Acknowledgments

First, and most of all, I thank my creator and savior, Jesus Christ. Without Him I could do nothing, and I know that every good thing I have comes from Him (James 1:17). I am also very grateful to the many individuals who helped bring this book about and/or make it better. This book has been a family project, but there wasn't room on the cover to put all of our names. My wonderful wife, Debbie, and our crew: Zachary, Abigail, Benjamin, Sarah, Solomon, Hannah, Joanna, Rebekah, Susanna, Noah, Samuel, Gideon, and Joshua all helped in various ways from proofreading/editing to just cheering me up and keeping me going. Thank you, and I love you all very much.

The technical reviewers, beta readers, and others who provided feedback have made this book much better than I ever could have done on my own. Aitor Alzola, Jeff Brown, Doug Burns, Frederick Daoud, Scott Davis, Paolo Foletto, Amer Ghumrawi, Bill Gloff, Brian Grant, Steve Harris, Brian Hogan, Dmitriy Kopylenko, Guillaume Laforge, Shih-gian Lee, John Penrod, Jared Richardson, Nathaniel Schutta, Ken Sipe, Dan Sline, Matt Stine, Venkat Subramaniam, and Ray Tayek: thank you all so much for your help and encouragement!

Writing a book for the Pragmatic Programmers has been an awesome experience, and I am very grateful to them for giving me this opportunity. Dave, Andy, Colleen, Jackie, and Susannah: working with you has been an honor, a privilege, and a lot of fun! I can't wait to do it again!

Many others helped bring this book about in various ways, though they may not know it. I'd like to thank the gang at the Culver's in Portage, Wisconsin, for their cheerful faces, for their free wireless, and for not chasing me out even after closing time. To the speakers on the NoFluffJustStuff symposium tour and Jay Zimmerman, their ringleader: thank you for your inspiration, encouragement, and example! Matthew Porter, Craig McElroy, and the rest of the gang at Contegix: thank you for giving me the opportunity to spend some time at such an exciting company and for your continued support of the Grails community. I'd also like to thank my former co-worker (and the best programmer in the world) Nate Neff for attempting to temper my enthusiasm (it's not gonna work).

Finally, I'd like to thank the Grails development team and the Grails community for making web development so much fun.

Tell me and I forget. Teach me and I remember. Involve me and I learn.
► Benjamin Franklin

Chapter 2

Our Project

When you're learning a new tool or language, you might start with a "Hello World" example or perhaps work through a few exercises in a book. Those steps can help you become acquainted with the tool, but that's as far as they'll take you. If you want to become productive in a tool or even proficient, you need use it in a real project. So, that's what we're going to do. We'll work together to build a cool new web application—one that will actually go live. As our application comes together, we'll explore Grails in a thorough, practical way. This strategy will provide us with the context that is so valuable in understanding and becoming productive with a new framework.

We'll be working through a series of iterations, covering about one iteration per chapter. This means that some features of Grails will be used in more than one chapter. We want to build a real application, and the repetition that comes with that is a good thing. This is a quick-start guide, but we don't want it to be a false-start guide. When our time together is over, you'll be able to go on to your second Grails project with confidence.

One concern with this method of discovery is that we're going to run into more advanced features of Grails, perhaps before we are ready. We'll handle this potential problem by developing our application in an incremental manner. In other words, our application will start simple, thereby exercising the simple features in Grails, and gradually get more complex.

2.1 Introducing TekDays.com

The decision about what kind of project to take on in our quest to learn Grails is an important one. We want something that is substantial enough to exercise the framework in ways that will stick in our minds but not something that is so daunting that we are unable to finish it. We're also aiming for something useful *and* interesting. After all, you may need something more than my charm and wit to keep your attention.

Here's an issue many developers encounter: the rapid pace of techno-logical innovation today is making it more difficult and, at the same time, increasingly important to keep our skills as developers up-to-date. One great way to keep on top of innovations and advances is to attend technical conferences, but with tightening training budgets at many companies and more developers working as freelancers or inde-pendent contractors, it is often hard to afford these events. Some devel-opers have taken to organizing local, nonprofit mini-conferences to help address the problem. You may have heard of these events, such as the Houston Tech Fest, Silicon Valley Code Camp, or the bar camps that are springing up all over.[1] Wouldn't it be great if there was an online appli-cation to help individuals connect and put on these types of events? Well, when we're done here, there will be.

TekDays.com is going to be a site where people can announce, plan, and promote local, grassroots technical conferences. It will all start when visionary individuals suggest an event in their city. Then, as oth-ers hear about it and register their interest and/or support, we'll pro-vide tools to help them organize the event: a to-do list, an organizer's dashboard (to keep track of volunteers, sponsors, and potential atten-dees), a discussion forum, and, finally, a customizable event page to help with promotion. This may sound like a tall order, but Grails can make it happen.

2.2 Meet Our Customer

One of the major benefits of Grails is its ability to provide rapid feed-back. In minutes, we can have new features up and running and ready for our customers to try. But that benefit is hard to realize if we don't

---

1. For more information on these events, see http://www.houstontechfest.com, http://www.siliconvalley-codecamp.com, and http://en.wikipedia.org/wiki/BarCamp.

have a customer around. And this application is about building community: making connections, sharing ideas, and working together to build a solution. This application is going to production; in fact, I'm going to use it to organize a real tech conference, so I'll be joining you on the dev team as well as playing the role of on-site customer—*and* first end user. Don't worry; I have experience wearing multiple hats. As we work on TekDays, you can show me what you've done, and I'll let you know what I think about it. Fair enough?

Application Requirements

As your *customer*, I want to give you a good idea of what I am looking for in this application. I am trying to attract conference organizers to this site—preferably many of them. I am convinced of the value of these types of conferences to individual developers, communities, and the industry as a whole. The application should make it easy for those visionary individuals to get started by simply proposing a conference. Then it has to provide real help in bringing their vision to fruition.

As an *end user*, I am hoping to use this application to organize a technical conference in St. Louis, Missouri. This is a big undertaking, and I know that I can't do it alone, so I need this application to make it easy for others to volunteer, or to at least let me know that they are interested in attending. Some type of workflow to guide me through the process would make this whole endeavor much less daunting.

After this introduction and a follow-up discussion with our customer and user (me and myself, respectively), we have come up with the following feature list for our application:

- Create new events

- Display event details

- Edit event details

- Create users/organizers

- Allow users to volunteer to help

- Add users to events

- Allow anonymous users to register interest

- Create sponsors

- Add sponsors to events

- Have default list of tasks

- Add/remove tasks

- Assign tasks to users

- Post forum message

- Reply to forum message

- Display forum message threads

- Customize event page

- Allow access to event home page with simple URL

This list gives us a good idea of the scope of the project. When we're done here, people will be able to propose conferences, volunteer to help, or add their support. Organizers will be able to assign tasks to volunteers to spread the load, and questions can be asked and answered in the forums to keep the communication flowing. As a conference begins to take shape, we'll provide the tools needed to promote it successfully. Businesses will be able to bring their resources to bear to help make it all happen. This is getting exciting!

We will, of course, need to flesh these out more as we go along. During each iteration, we'll design and implement two or three features. Along the way, we (or our customer) may come up with new features or changes. That's OK. Grails can handle it, and so can we.

2.3 Iteration Zero

Before we get started building our application, we'll take a few moments to set the stage.

Installing Grails

First off, let's get Grails installed and set up. There are a few different ways to install Grails, with installers on one end of the spectrum and building the source out of SVN on the other. We'll use that happy middle ground and download the compressed binaries. They are at http://grails. org/download and come in either zip or tar/gz versions. Once we have them, follow these steps:

1. Expand the archive to a directory on your computer.

2. Set your GRAILS_HOME environment variable to this directory.

3. Add GRAILS_HOME/bin to your path.

4. Ensure that you have a JAVA_HOME environment variable pointing to a JDK version 1.5 or higher.

To test our installation, run the following command:

```
$ grails help
```

If this returns something like the following output, then we're good to go:

```
Welcome to Grails 1.1 - http://grails.org/
Licensed under Apache Standard License 2.0
Grails home is set to: /opt/grails/current

Base Directory: /Users/dave/dev
Running script /opt/grails/current/scripts/Help_.groovy
Environment set to development

Usage (optionals marked with *):
grails [environment]* [target] [arguments]*

Examples:
grails dev run-app
grails create-app books

Available Targets (type grails help 'target-name' for more info):
grails bootstrap
grails bug-report
grails clean
grails compile
grails console
grails create-app
grails create-controller
grails create-domain-class
grails create-filters
grails create-integration-test
...
```

If you don't see this output, verify that your GRAILS_HOME and JAVA_HOME environment variables are valid and that GRAILS_HOME/bin is on your path. You can do this easily with echo:

```
$ echo $GRAILS_HOME
$ echo $JAVA_HOME
$ echo $PATH
```

On Windows, this would be as follows:

```
> echo %GRAILS_HOME%
> echo %JAVA_HOME%
> echo %PATH%
```

Grails Scripts

Grails comes with more than forty built-in scripts that can be run with the grails command. These scripts are used for creating applications and application artifacts, as well as to run tests or to run the application. We'll learn about many of these as we work on TekDays. If you want to explore the others, you can do that with grails help. As we saw in the previous section, grails help will show you a list of the scripts that come with the framework. To find out more about any one of them, run grails help followed by the name of the script. For example:

```
$ grails help run-app
```

Although we will be using the built-in scripts only to get TekDays ready for production, it's worth noting that other scripts can be used with the grails command; some plug-ins install new scripts, and it's also possible to write your own scripts for Grails.

Setting Up Our Workspace

In other web frameworks that I've used—especially Java-based frameworks—starting a new project is an ordeal. If you're lucky, there might be a wizard, or perhaps there's a template project you can copy and customize. Even with those aids, getting everything set up and in the right place can be a drag. Grails has a solution to this problem, in the form of a script called create-app. We'll use this script to get TekDays off the ground.

From the directory that will be the parent of our project directory, enter the following command:

```
$ grails create-app TekDays
```

The output of this script shows us that Grails is creating a bunch of directories and files for our project. In just a bit, we'll take a closer look at the directories that are created and what they are used for.

The TekDays project is now ready to go. In fact, we can even run it already:

```
$ cd TekDays
$ grails run-app
```

Here's a summarized view of the output from the run-app script:

```
Base Directory: /Users/dave/dev/TekDays
Running script /opt/grails/current/scripts/RunApp.groovy
Environment set to development
Running Grails application..
Server running. Browse to http://localhost:8080/TekDays
```

Figure 2.1: WE START WITH A WORKING APPLICATION.

Grails gives us some directory information and then tells us that the environment is set to development. development is the default of the three standard Grails environments. Running in the development environment (or in development mode, as it is often called) gives us auto-reloading (we can change most aspects of the application while it's running and see the changes immediately) and an in-memory database to make that rapid feedback even more rapid. These types of productivity-enhancing features can be added to most other frameworks via external tools and libraries, but Grails bakes them right in. The other two environments are test and prod. We'll return to these other environments later when we get to testing and deployment. For now, keep in mind that these are only defaults and can be changed if needed. The last line of output tells us where to go to see our application in action. In Figure 2.1, we can see what we get by browsing to that location.

It may not look like much yet, but having a working application from the very beginning is just *powerful*. It gives us an excellent feedback loop. We'll be maintaining that runnable state, and, consequently, that feedback loop, right through to deployment.

Starting with All Windows Intact

In their book *The Pragmatic Programmer* (HT00), Dave Thomas and Andy Hunt discuss the "Broken Window" theory as it relates to software development. This theory holds that if a building has a broken window that is left unrepaired, its chances of further vandalism are increased. Dave and Andy point out that if software is left in a partially broken state (failing tests or ignored bugs), it will continue to degenerate.

With many development tools and frameworks, we start out with broken windows; nothing works until multiple pieces are in place. This makes it easier to get started and keep coding without taking the time to see whether what we have *works*. With Grails we start out with a running application; as we make changes, we get immediate feedback that lets us know whether we've broken something.

With some other web frameworks, we would have had to create one or two source files, an index page, and a handful of XML files to get this far. All it took in Grails was a single command.

Anatomy of a Grails Project

Now that we've seen our application run, let's take a look at what's under the hood. When we ran the create-app script, several files and directories were generated for us. (See Figure 2.2, on the facing page.) The files that were created have default code and configuration information that we can change as needed. The directories are particularly important because they are at the heart of Grails' "convention over configuration" strategy. Each directory has a purpose, and when files are placed in these directories and meet certain other conventions, *magical things* will happen. We will look at most of these in more detail when we begin to work with them. For now, here's a brief overview:

- grails-app: The main application directory. It contains the following directories:
    - conf: Contains Grails configuration files and directories for optional Hibernate and Spring configuration files[2]

---

2. Most Grails applications will not need Spring or Hibernate configuration files.

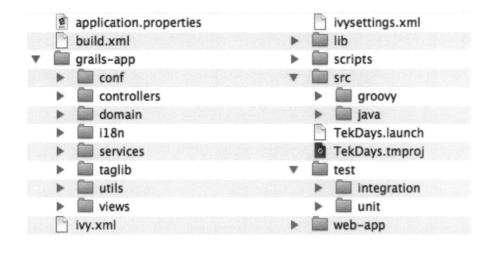

Figure 2.2: THE FILES AND DIRECTORIES OF A GRAILS APPLICATION

- controllers: Holds the controller classes, the entry points into a Grails application

- domain: Holds domain classes, representing persistent data

- i18n: Holds message property files for internationalization

- services: Holds service classes, which are Spring-managed beans

- taglib: Holds Groovy Server Pages (GSP) custom tag libraries

- utils: Holds codec classes[3]

- views: Holds the GSP views

- lib: Contains any external .jar files we may need to include (such as JDBC drivers).

- scripts: Can contain custom Groovy scripts to be used in the application.

- src: Contains directories for other Java and Groovy source files. Files in this directory are available to the application at runtime.

- test: Contains directories for unit and integration tests.

- web-app: Contains directories for images, CSS, and JavaScript.

---

3.   See http://www.grails.org/Dynamic+Encoding+Methods.

There are also a few files shown in Figure 2.2, on the previous page. Most of them are there to make it easier to work with a Grails project using other tools, which you may or may not choose to explore. The application.properties file holds our application's name and version, along with a list of plug-ins used. The default version for a new Grails application is 0.1; we can change this in application.properties.

Speaking of other tools, the support for Groovy and Grails in most of the popular development tools is good and getting better all the time. Integrated development environments (IDEs) such as Eclipse, NetBeans, and IntelliJ IDEA are a big help in managing a multitude of configuration files or for dealing with verbose and redundant language syntax, but with Grails' use of "convention over configuration" and the clean, concise syntax of Groovy, I find myself turning to an IDE less and less. If you really feel the need for an IDE, you can find more information about what's available in Appendix B, on page 203. As we work on Tek-Days, we will be using the command line for interacting with Grails, but coding can be done in an editor or IDE.

2.4 Summary

We're off to a good start. We have Grails installed. Our project requirements are clear and achievable. Our new application is prepped, ready, and running.

In the next chapter, we'll begin our first development iteration. To get ourselves acclimated, we'll reach for some low-hanging fruit and work on the first three features on our list. At the end of Chapter 3, we will be able to create, display, and edit an event.

Chapter 3

Laying the Foundation

In this chapter, we'll implement the first three features on the TekDays feature list. We'll add the ability to create, view, and modify new technical conferences (or code camps or what have you). We will refer to all of these as *events*. These events are the core of our application. Each event that is created here has the potential to become an actual gathering of dozens, if not hundreds, of developers, designers, architects, and maybe even project managers, all learning, sharing, and generally advancing our craft.

The three features that we'll be implementing are very closely related; they're so close, in fact, that we will be implementing them all at once! Grails dynamically adds the ability to create, read, update, and delete data from a *domain class*. We will take advantage of this to get us started, but we won't stop there.

3.1 Creating a Domain Class

The heart of a Grails application is its *domain model*, that is, the set of domain classes and their relationships.

A domain class represents *persistent data* and, by default, is used to create a table in a database. We'll talk more about this shortly when we create our first domain class. For creating domain classes, Grails provides a convenience script called (unsurprisingly)[1] create-domain-class.

---

1. The designers of Grails followed the *principle of least surprise*; most names in Grails are common sense and therefore easy to remember.

```
            TekEvent
String city
String name
TekUser organizer
String venue
Date startDate
Date endDate
String description
```

Figure 3.1: DIAGRAM OF THE TEKEVENT CLASS

Just as the domain model is the heart of a Grails application, the TekEvent class will be the heart of the TekDays domain model. TekEvent is the name of the class that we will use to represent an event (or conference or code camp or tech fest). If we were to sit down and put our heads together to come up with a design for the TekEvent class, we'd probably end up with something similar to what we see in Figure 3.1.

To create our TekEvent class, run the following command:

```
$ grails create-domain-class TekEvent
```

The output from this command has a few lines of introductory text and then these two lines:

```
Created DomainClass for TekEvent
Created Tests for TekEvent
```

Grails created two files for us: the domain class and a unit test class. This is an example of the way that Grails makes it easier for us to do the right thing. We still need to add tests, but having this test class already created for us gives us a little nudge in the right direction.

In Grails, a domain class is a Groovy class located in grails-app/domain. Let's take a look:

```
class TekEvent {

    static constraints = {
    }
}
```

Pretty anemic, huh? Grails is powerful but not omniscient. (Maybe in the next release....) We have to write a little code to make our TekEvent class useful. We'll use Groovy properties (see Section 1.7, *Groovy Syntax*

Compared to Java, on page 5.) to flesh out our domain class. It's time to fire up your trusty editor and add the following properties to the TekEvent class:

foundation/TekDays/grails-app/domain/TekEvent.groovy

```
String city
String name
String organizer
String venue
Date startDate
Date endDate
String description
```

We may need to come back to this class later and add or change things. In fact, I know we will. Notice that we gave our organizer property a type of String, but our diagram shows a User. That's because we don't have a User class yet. A look at our feature list shows us we will need one. But don't worry: refactoring a Grails application, especially in the early stages, is a breeze.

While you have your editor out, why not add a toString() method to TekEvent too? I find that this always comes in handy, since it gives us an easy way to represent an instance of our domain class as a String. We'll see later that Grails takes advantage of the toString() in the views that it generates, and if we don't create our own, we'll get Grails' default, which is not all that informative or user friendly.

Groovy makes this very easy to do. Add the following code after the properties we just added:

foundation/TekDays/grails-app/domain/TekEvent.groovy

```
String toString(){
    "$name, $city"
}
```

This toString() method will return the name and city of the TekEvent separated by a comma. For a refresher on what's going on here, take another look at Section 1.7, *Groovy Syntax Compared to Java*, on page 5 and Section 1.8, *Groovy Strings*, on page 7.

3.2 More About Domain Classes

Now we have a persistent TekEvent class. We can create instances of this class and save them to the database. We can even find existing instances by their id or by their properties. You might be wondering how that can be—where is the code for all this functionality?

> \\|/ **Joe Asks...**
> ‿͡
> **If Groovy Is a Dynamic Language, Why Are We Specifying the Types of Our Properties?**
>
> That's an excellent question. If you were creating a persistent class, why might you want to have data types on the properties? If your answer had something to do with the database schema, move to the head of the class! Groovy *is* a dynamic language, and our properties *could* be declared with the **def** keyword rather than a type, but by using types, Grails is able to tell our database what data type to use when defining columns. Grails also uses type information to choose default HTML elements for our views.

We'll learn more about that when we start using these features, but the short answer is that Grails dynamically adds powerful behavior to our domain classes. As we get further in developing our application, we'll see that we can call methods like TekEvent.save(), TekEvent.list(), and TekEvent.findAllByStartGreaterThan(new Date() - 30), even though we've never written any code to implement those methods.

Because domain classes are such an integral part of a Grails application, we will be coming back to them frequently as we work on TekDays, learning a bit more each time. There is, however, one more feature we should discuss before we continue. Along with dynamically adding several methods and nonpersistent properties to our domain classes, Grails adds two persistent properties: id and version. These properties are both Integers. The id property is the unique key in the table that is created, and the version is used by Grails for *optimistic concurrency*.[2]

3.3 Testing Our Domain Class

As I mentioned earlier, Grails makes it easy for us to do the right thing by generating test classes for us, but we still have to write the tests. So, let's add a test for our TekEvent class.

---

2. Optimistic concurrency is a way of keeping a user's changes from getting stomped on by another user changing the same data at the same time. It's outside the scope of this book, but see http://en.wikipedia.org/wiki/Optimistic_concurrency_control for more information.

> ## Testing and Dynamic Languages
>
> Writing automated tests for our code is always a good idea, but it becomes even more important when working with a dynamic language such as Groovy. In some situations, it's possible for a simple typo that would be caught by the Java compiler to sneak through and cause havoc at runtime. Automated unit tests can prevent that and much more. A compiler will verify that our code is syntactically correct, but a well-written test will verify that it works! As Stuart Halloway once said, "In five years, we will view compilation as a really weak form of unit testing."
>
> Fortunately, writing unit tests in Groovy is *much* easier than it would be in a language such as Java or C#. See Chapter 16, "Unit Testing and Mocking," in *Programming Groovy* (Sub08) for more information on applying the power of Groovy to unit testing.

Grails includes the JUnit testing framework wrapped in Groovy goodness. By default Grails provides two types of testing, *unit* and *integration*.[3] Since the goal of a unit test is to test a single class in isolation, Grails unit tests do not provide access to any of the dynamic behavior that would otherwise be available.

At this point, most of the functionality of the TekEvent class is dynamic. However, we can write a test for the toString() method. Open TekDays/test/unit/TekEventTests.groovy. You should see something like this:

```
import grails.test.*

class TekEventTests extends GrailsUnitTestCase {
    protected void setUp() {
        super.setUp()
    }

    protected void tearDown() {
        super.tearDown()
    }

    void testSomething() {

    }
}
```

---

3. We'll learn more about integration tests in Section 6.5, *Integration Testing*, on page 104.

Grails gives us one stubbed-out test called testSomething(). We can add as many tests as we want to a GrailsUnitTestCase; any method that begins with the word *test* will be treated as a test. We are currently adding only one test, so we will just replace testSomething() with a testToString() method. Modify the test class to look like this:

foundation/TekDays/test/unit/TekEventTests.groovy

```
import grails.test.*

class TekEventTests extends GrailsUnitTestCase {
    protected void setUp() {
        super.setUp()
    }

    protected void tearDown() {
        super.tearDown()
    }

  void testToString() {
    def tekEvent = new TekEvent(name: 'Groovy One',
                               city: 'San Francisco, CA',
                               organizer: 'John Doe',
                               venue: 'Moscone Center',
                               startDate: new Date('6/2/2009'),
                               endDate: new Date('6/5/2009'),
                               description: 'This conference will cover all...')
    assertEquals 'Groovy One, San Francisco, CA', tekEvent.toString()
  }
}
```

Our test code is simple enough. We are creating a new TekEvent using the named-args constructor, assigning it to the variable tekEvent, and asserting that tekEvent.toString() is equal to the expected value.

Grails provides a script called test-app that will, by default, run all of our application's unit and integration tests. We can use the -unit flag to tell it to run only unit tests. This is helpful since we want to run our tests frequently and unit tests are much faster than integration tests. Let's use it now to run our test:

```
$ grails test-app -unit
```

In the output from this command, we see the following lines:

```
Running 1 Unit Test...
Running test TekEventTests...
                testToString...SUCCESS
Unit Tests Completed in 409ms ...
...
Tests PASSED - view reports in .../iteration_1/TekDays/test/reports.
```

Each TestCase is shown, and each individual test is listed with its result. The result will be either SUCCESS, FAILURE, or ERROR. FAILURE means that the test ran with one or more assertion failures. ERROR means that an exception occurred. In the event of a FAILURE or ERROR, you will find very helpful information in the HTML reports that Grails produces. The final line of output from test-app gives the location of these reports.

3.4 Taking Control of Our Domain

The next step in implementing our first features is to give our users a way to create TekEvent instances. To do this, we will need a *controller* class. Controller classes are the dispatchers of a Grails application. All requests from the browser come through a controller. We will do quite a bit of work with controller classes later, but for now all we need is a blank one. Once again, Grails has a script to produce this:

```
$ grails create-controller TekEvent
```

This will create the files grails-app/controllers/TekEventController.groovy and test/unit/TekEventControllerTests.groovy. (We won't be using the TestCase yet since we currently have virtually no code to test.) Let's open the TekEvent-Controller in our editor and take a look:

```
class TekEventController {

    def index = { }
}
```

The line that we see in this otherwise empty controller—def index = { }—is called an *action*. Specifically, the index action. We will eventually have controllers full of actions, but for now we will take advantage of a powerful Grails feature called *dynamic scaffolding*. Dynamic scaffolding will generate a controller with a set of actions and corresponding views (pages), which we will discuss shortly. To get all this magic, let's change the TekEventController to look like this:

foundation/TekDays/grails-app/controllers/TekEventController.groovy

```
class TekEventController {

    def scaffold = TekEvent

}
```

Now when we run our application, we see a link titled TekEventController on the index page. This link takes us to the *list* view. This is

Figure 3.2: THE SCAFFOLDED LIST VIEW

the first of four views that are made available by the dynamic scaffolding; the others are *create*, *edit*, and *show*. Run the application, navigate to http://localhost:8080/TekDays, and click the TekEventController link. You should see something like Figure 3.2.

The list is (obviously) empty, since we haven't created any events yet. In the menu bar of the list view, there is a button labeled New TekEvent. This button will take us to the create view. (See Figure 3.3, on the next page.) We'll have to tweak these views a bit, but first let's see what our customer thinks.

3.5 Modifying Code That Doesn't Exist

I put on my customer hat, and, after getting over my shock at how fast you got this much done, I found the following issues with these views:

- List view:

  - The Grails logo, while very cool, is not the logo I had in mind for TekDays.

  - The id column is not something that I or other users need to see.

Figure 3.3: THE SCAFFOLDED CREATE VIEW

– What's with the order of the columns? I would prefer to see Name, City, Description, Organizer, Venue, and so on.

- Create view:

  – The logo and field order issues apply here too.

  – There is definitely not enough room in the Description field to enter any meaningful content.

  – I don't need to enter the minutes and seconds of an event's start and end dates.

Some of these issues will have to wait until we generate code that we can modify.[4] Currently we are using *dynamic scaffolding*, which allows us to make changes to our domain model and quickly see the effects of those changes but doesn't provide us with any code that we can customize. However, we can fix some of the issues the customer brought up by modifying our TekEvent class.

Constraining Our Domain

Grails uses our domain classes to make some decisions about the scaffolding. For example, property types are used to determine which HTML elements to use. To go further, we can add *constraints* to our domain class. Constraints are a way of telling Grails more about the properties of our domain class. They are used for validation when saving, for determining some aspects of database schema generation, and for laying out scaffolded views. We'll look at those first two uses of constraints later (see the sidebar on page 66), but that last one is what we're going to take advantage of now. Open TekDays/grails-app/domain/TekEvent.groovy in your trusty editor, and add the following code:

foundation/TekDays/grails-app/domain/TekEvent.groovy

```
static constraints = {
    name()
    city()
    description(maxSize:5000)
    organizer()
    venue()
    startDate()
    endDate()
}
```

The constraints consist of a code block, which is a Groovy closure.[5] Inside this block, we list each of our properties, followed by parentheses. Inside the parentheses, we can include one or more key/value pairs that represent rules for that property. The order of the properties in the constraints block will be used to determine the display order in the scaffolded views. The maxSize constraint that we added to the description property will affect how that property is displayed in the views and will also affect the database schema generation. For example, in MySQL,[6]

---

4. Grails does provide a way to make more significant changes to dynamically scaffolded views with the install-templates script. You can read about it at http://grails.org/Artifact+and+Scaffolding+Templates.

5. See Section 1.9, *Groovy Closures*, on page 8.

6. See http://dev.mysql.com.

Figure 3.4: LIST VIEW WITH CONSTRAINTS

the description field will be of type TEXT, whereas nonconstrained String properties will render fields of VARCHAR(255).

When we run the application and navigate to the list view, we see that it looks more like Figure 3.4. In this view, we corrected only the order of the properties, but if we click the New TekEvent button, we see that the create page looks significantly better. (See Figure 3.5, on the next page.) The order of the properties is correct, and we get a text area for entering a description instead of an input field. We haven't addressed all the issues yet, but we're moving in the right direction, and we'll continue to make small corrections as we go.

3.6 Bootstrapping Some Test Data

To get a better feel for how TekDays is coming along, we can enter some data and check out the various views. We've seen the list and create views, but there's also the show and edit views.

The problem with entering test data now is that it would all be lost as soon as we restarted the application. We're working with an *in-memory database* at this point. Eventually, we will point TekDays at a real database, but for now, the in-memory HSQL database is pretty handy—that is, it would be if we didn't lose our data.

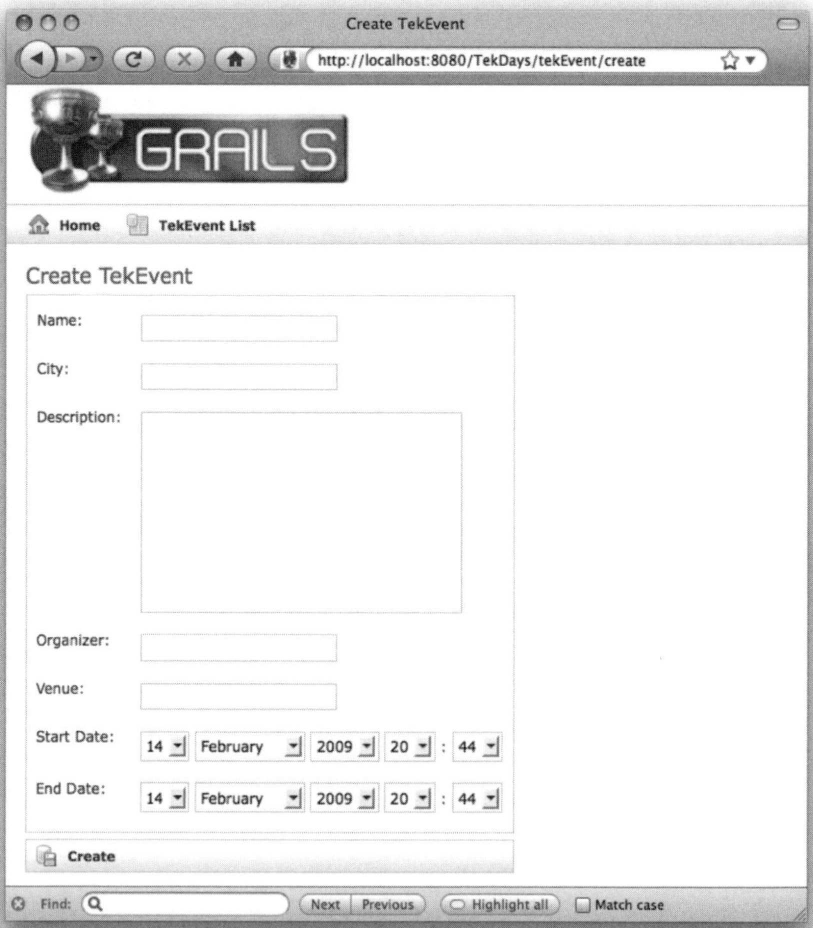

Figure 3.5: CREATE VIEW WITH CONSTRAINTS

This dilemma's answer is in TekDays/grails-app/conf/BootStrap.groovy. The file has an init() code block, which is executed by our application at start-up. If we create TekEvent instances there, they will be preloaded for us every time we run the application. (Once we do set up a persistent database, we'll tweak this code to make sure we don't get duplicates.)

Give it a try. Open TekDays/grails-app/conf/BootStrap.groovy, and modify it to look similar to the following code. You can make up your own event. Be creative. It makes the learning process more fun.

foundation/TekDays/grails-app/conf/BootStrap.groovy

```groovy
class BootStrap {

    def init = { servletContext ->
        def event1 = new TekEvent(name: 'Gateway Code Camp',
                    city: 'Saint Louis, MO',
                    organizer: 'John Doe',
                    venue: 'TBD',
                    startDate: new Date('9/19/2009'),
                    endDate: new Date('9/19/2009'),
                    description: '''This conference will bring coders from
                                across platforms, languages, and industries
                                together for an exciting day of tips, tricks,
                                and tech!  Stay sharp! Stay at the top of your
                                game!  But, don't stay home!  Come an join us
                                this fall for the first annual Gateway Code
                                Camp.''')
        if (!event1.save()){
            event1.errors.allErrors.each{error ->
                println "An error occured with event1: ${error}"
            }
        }

        def event2 = new TekEvent(name: 'Perl Before Swine',
                    city: 'Austin, MN',
                    organizer: 'John Deere',
                    venue: 'SPAM Museum',
                    startDate: new Date('9/1/2009'),
                    endDate: new Date('9/1/2009'),
                    description: '''Join the Perl programmers of the Pork Producers
                                of America as we hone our skills and ham it up
                                a bit.  You can show off your programming chops
                                while trying to win a year's supply of pork
                                chops in our programming challenge.

                                Come and join us in historic (and aromatic),
                                Austin, Minnesota.  You'll know when you're
                                there!''')
```

```
            if (!event2.save()){
                    event2.errors.allErrors.each{error ->
                            println "An error occured with event2: ${error}"
                    }
            }
    }
}

    def destroy = {
    }
}
```

Notice the triple single quotes ('") surrounding the description values in our new TekEvent instances. This is a Groovy way to declare a multiline String, which allows us to enter text on multiple lines without joining them with **+** signs. (It's yet another way that Groovy helps us keep our code cleaner.)

By assigning our new TekEvent instances to a variable and then saving them in a separate step, we're able to do a little error checking in case we mistyped something; when a domain class instance fails to save, its errors property will be populated with one or more Error objects, which will give us some clues as to what went wrong.

Once you've saved those changes, run the application again. When we navigate to the list view, it should look more like Figure 3.6, on page 42. If your new data doesn't show up, check your console output to see whether anything was reported by our sophisticated error-handling system.

```
if (!event1.save()){
    event1.errors.allErrors.each{error ->
        println "An error occured with event1: ${error}"
    }
}
```

Now that we have some data to look at, I'd like to point out a couple more features of the default list view. The id property in the first column is, by default, a link that will bring up the selected item in the show view. We will change this once we have generated code to work with, but for now it's an easy way to get around. The other feature is difficult to show on a printed page: all the columns in the table are sortable by clicking the column header. The sort order will toggle between ascending and descending as you would expect. Not bad for the amount of code we had to write!

> ### Joe Asks...
> #### Why Not Just Use a "Real" Database from the Beginning?
>
> When your Grails application is hooked up to a persistent database, it becomes a little more difficult to make changes to the domain model. Grails will make some updates to your database; for example, it will add new columns based on new properties. But it won't drop columns.
>
> Using the in-memory database for development makes it easier to share your project with other developers, since they don't have to create a database to run your project locally. And if you're working on a team, using the in-memory database with test data loaded in BootStrap.groovy can prevent issues with tests passing on one machine and not another because of data differences.
>
> If you prefer to not use the in-memory database for development, you can jump ahead to Section 5.4, *Configuring a Database*, on page 86 for information on hooking up to a MySQL database, in which case you can skip the Boot-Strap.groovy code altogether.

3.7 Summary

We're off to a great start. We have the basics of the first three features working: we can create new events, we can edit them (see Figure 3.8, on page 44), and we can display them (see Figure 3.7, on page 43). Our customer is still a little skeptical about how the views look, but we'll smooth things over. In the meantime, let's press on with the next two features. In the next chapter, we're going to add users and allow them to volunteer for events.

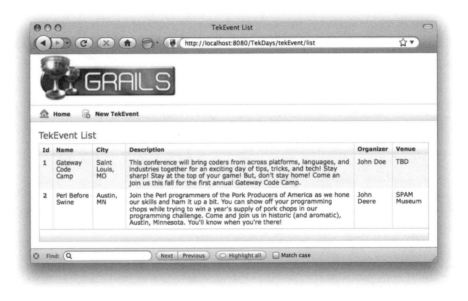

Figure 3.6: LIST VIEW WITH SAMPLE DATA

Figure 3.7: TEKEVENT SHOW VIEW

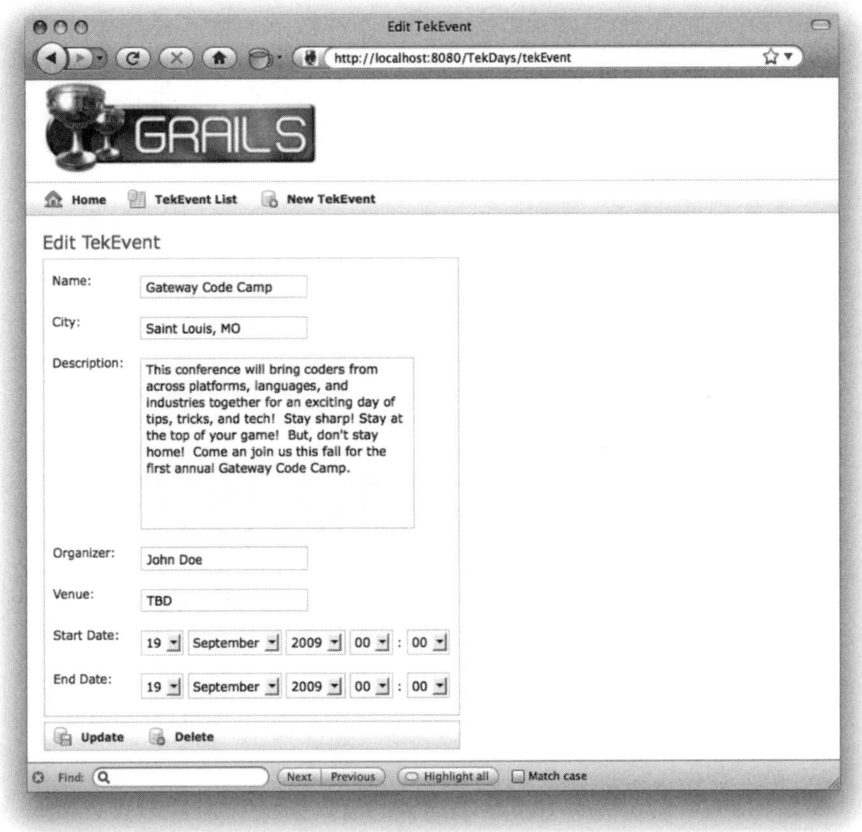

Figure 3.8: TEKEVENT EDIT VIEW

Chapter 4

Building Relationships

In this iteration, we will be adding more domain classes and defining the relationships between them.

The *event* is key to the TekDays application, but we can't have an event without that visionary individual who steps up to organize it and the enthusiastic volunteers who help bring it about. *Organizers* and *volunteers* are two roles that *users* of TekDays will play. The same user can be an organizer of one event and a volunteer on one or more others. The TekDays domain model will have to reflect these relationships, but it takes more than one to form a relationship. So, we'll start by adding another domain class.

4.1 The TekUser Domain Class

Some databases consider User to be a reserved word, so we'll call our class TekUser. (Kind of catchy, huh?) Our TekUser class diagram looks like this:

TekUser
String fullName
String userName
String password
String email
String website
String bio

To create this class, we'll run the create-domain-class script like so:

```
$ grails create-domain-class TekUser
```

Now open TekDays/grails-app/domain/TekUser.groovy, and edit it to look like this:

model/TekDays/grails-app/domain/TekUser.groovy

```
class TekUser {
    String fullName
    String userName
    String password
    String email
    String website
    String bio

    String toString(){ fullName }

    static constraints = {
        fullName()
        userName()
        email()
        website()
        bio(maxSize:5000)
    }
}
```

We added the constraints and toString() method right away this time. Next, we'll create the controller and enable dynamic scaffolding for our TekUser class. Go ahead and run grails create-controller:

```
$ grails create-controller TekUser
```

Now let's enable the scaffolding:

model/TekDays/grails-app/controllers/TekUserController.groovy

```
class TekUserController {

    def scaffold = TekUser
}
```

This gives us scaffolded views, like the ones we saw for TekEvent. Before we look at those, let's go ahead and add some test data to make them more interesting. Open TekDays/grails-app/conf/BootStrap.groovy, and add the following code to the init block immediately after the code we added in the previous chapter:

model/TekDays/grails-app/conf/BootStrap.groovy

```
new TekUser(fullName: 'John Doe',
            userName: 'jdoe',
            password: 't0ps3cr3t',
            email: 'jdoe@johnsgroovyshop.com',
```

```
            website: 'blog.johnsgroovyshop.com',
            bio: '''John has been programming for over 40 years.  He has worked
                   with every programming language known to man and has settled
                   on Groovy.  In his spare time, John dabbles in astro physics
                   and plays shuffleboard.''').save()

new TekUser(fullName: 'John Deere',
            userName: 'tractorman',
            password: 't0ps3cr3t',
            email: 'john.deere@porkproducers.org',
            website: 'www.perl.porkproducers.org',
            bio: '''John is a top notch Perl programmer and a pretty good
                   hand around the farm.  If he can't program it he can
                   plow it!''').save()
```

This code is similar to our test data for TekEvent, so we won't spend much time on it.

Now when we run TekDays and navigate to the index page, we see a new link for the TekUserController. Follow this link to see the list view, as shown in Figure 4.1, on the following page.

The generated list views don't show all the properties of our class; by default, the Grails scaffolding produces list views with six columns. The first column will always be the id property, which Grails added to our domain. The rest of the columns are chosen based on the current ordering of properties. (Remember that the property ordering is alphabetical by default but can be changed by adding constraints, as we discussed in Section 3.5, *Constraining Our Domain*, on page 36.)

Now that we have two domain classes, we can see how Grails handles domain relationships.

4.2 One-to-One Relationships

In Figure 3.1, on page 28, the organizer property is shown as a TekUser, but in our current TekEvent, it's still a String. Now that we have a TekUser, we can fix this discrepancy. Let's open TekDays/grails-app/domain/TekEvent.groovy and change the organizer from a String to a TekUser:

model/TekDays/grails-app/domain/TekEvent.groovy

```
    String city
    String name
►   TekUser organizer
    String venue
    Date startDate
    Date endDate
    String description
```

Figure 4.1: TEKUSER LIST VIEW

We have now joined the TekEvent and TekUser classes in a *one-to-one* relationship. Each TekEvent instance can have exactly one TekUser. That was simple enough; however, if we save this and try to run our application, we'll get a lovely (and long) error stacktrace. The problem is that we are still assigning a String ('John Doe' or 'John Deere') to the organizer property of the TekEvent instances that we created in BootStrap.groovy. This will be easy to fix, but we will need to do a bit more coding.

In the init block of BootStrap.groovy, we are creating two TekEvent instances and two TekUser instances. We are creating them anonymously and then saving them to the database so that they are available to the rest of the application. Let's take advantage of this: we can retrieve the TekUser objects from the database and assign them to the organizer property of our TekEvent instances. For this to work, we'll also have to rearrange our code so that the TekUser instances are created first. Here's an abbreviated version of what this should look like:

```
model.1/TekDays/grails-app/conf/BootStrap.groovy

def init = { servletContext ->
    new TekUser(fullName: 'John Doe',
                userName: 'jdoe',
                password: 't0ps3cr3t',
                email: 'jdoe@johnsgroovyshop.com',
```

```
                        website: 'blog.johnsgroovyshop.com',
                        bio: 'John has been programming for over 40 years. ...').save()
        new TekUser(fullName: 'John Deere',
                    userName: 'tractorman',
                    password: 't0ps3cr3t',
                    email: 'john.deere@porkproducers.org',
                    website: 'www.perl.porkproducers.org',

                    bio: 'John is a top notch Perl programmer and a ...').save()

        new TekEvent(name: 'Gateway Code Camp',
                     city: 'Saint Louis, MO',
                     organizer: TekUser.findByFullName('John Doe'),
                     venue: 'TBD',
                     startDate: new Date('9/19/2009'),
                     endDate: new Date('9/19/2009'),
                     description: 'This conference will bring coders ...').save()
        new TekEvent(name: 'Perl Before Swine',
                     city: 'Austin, MN',
                     organizer: TekUser.findByFullName('John Deere'),
                     venue: 'SPAM Museum',
                     startDate: new Date('9/1/2009'),
                     endDate: new Date('9/1/2009'),
                     description: 'Join the Perl programmers of the ...').save()
    }
```

Introducing GORM

What we just did is almost trivial as far as code goes but very interesting behind the scenes. To set the value for the organizer property of each TekEvent, we are calling the method TekUser.findByFullName(). This method doesn't actually exist. I mentioned earlier that Grails adds methods to our domain classes at runtime. This is not one of them. Instead, what Grails is doing here is *synthesizing behavior at runtime*. When a method call beginning with *findBy* is made on one of our domain classes, Grails will parse the rest of the method name to see whether it matches any of the properties of the class. Then it executes the behavior that we would expect if a method with that name and parameters did exist. This is called a *dynamic finder*, and it is part of one of Grails' core components called Grails Object Relational Mapping (GORM).

Any time we save, retrieve, or relate any of our domain class instances, we are using GORM. GORM removes the need for much of the boilerplate, repetitive code that we would have to write to work with other ORM systems or JDBC.[1] We'll learn more about GORM and take advantage of more of its features as we continue working on TekDays.

---

1. Java Database Connectivity.

<u>**Dynamic Finders**</u>

Grails takes advantage of Groovy's metaprogramming capabilities to *synthesize* finders for our domain class properties at runtime.* We can call methods that begin with *findBy*, *findAllBy*, or *countBy*, followed by up to two properties and optional operators.

Some examples will make this clearer. All of these would be valid methods on a TekEvent instance:

- countByCity('New York')
- findAllByStartDateGreaterThan(new Date())
- findByCityAndDescriptionLike("Minneapolis", "%Groovy%")

Properties in dynamic finders can be joined by And or Or. The following are some of the operators that can be used:

- LessThan
- Between
- IsNotNull
- Like

For the complete list of operators, see http://www.grails.org/OperatorNamesInDynamicMethods.

---

*. For more information about metaprogramming in Groovy, see http://groovy.codehaus.org/Dynamic+Groovy.

The code we added hooks up TekEvent and TekUser in a unidirectional one-to-one relationship. A TekEvent *has a* TekUser, but the TekUser doesn't know anything about the TekEvent.

Now that we have a domain relationship, let's take a look at it. Run the application, and follow the TekEventController link. Then click the id of one of the rows to bring up the show view. It should look similar to what is shown in Figure 4.2, on the next page. Notice that the organizer's full name now appears as a link. This link takes us to the TekUser show view.

Keeping Our Tests Updated

If we've been running our tests frequently with grails test-app (and we should be), we will see that our TekEventTests fails.

Figure 4.2: TekEvent show view with link to TekUser

That's because the test code still expects TekEvent.organizer to be a String. Let's fix that before we move on.

We don't really want to include the TekUser class in the unit test for TekEvent, so instead, we'll mock the organizer with a Map. Open Tek-Days/test/unit/TekEventTests.groovy, and change the organizer property, as shown here:

model.1/TekDays/test/unit/TekEventTests.groovy

```
import grails.test.*

class TekEventTests extends GrailsUnitTestCase {
    protected void setUp() {
        super.setUp()
    }

    protected void tearDown() {
        super.tearDown()
    }
```

```
    void testToString() {
      def tekEvent = new TekEvent(name: 'Groovy One',
                                  city: 'San Francisco, CA',
                                  organizer: [fullName:'John Doe'] as TekUser,
                                  venue: 'Moscone Center',
                                  startDate: new Date('6/2/2009'),
                                  endDate: new Date('6/5/2009'),
                                  description: 'This conference will cover all...')
      assertEquals 'Groovy One, San Francisco, CA', tekEvent.toString()
    }
}
```

Groovy allows us to coerce a Map to a class or interface with the **as** operator. We're giving the Map a firstName element for clarity, but we could just as well have used an empty Map, since we're not referring to any of the organizer's properties in our test.

Now our tests pass. All is well.

4.3 One-to-Many Relationships

A TekEvent will have one organizer but will need more than one volunteer to be successful. A volunteer is also a TekUser, and we just set up a relationship between TekEvent and TekUser. We're going to set up another relationship between these two classes, but this time it will be a one-to-many relationship. A TekEvent will have zero or more volunteers.

Grails uses a static property called hasMany to declare one-to-many relationships. hasMany is a Map, with the key being the name of the collection in the owning class and the value being the type of the child class. Let's see how that looks in our TekEvent. Open TekDays/grails-app/domain/TekEvent.groovy, and add the hasMany declaration, as shown in the following code:

model/TekDays/grails-app/domain/TekEvent.groovy
```
    Date endDate
    String description
    static hasMany = [volunteers : TekUser]
    String toString(){
        "$name, $city"
    }
```

That line of code—static hasMany = [volunteers : TekUser]—gives us a Collection of TekUser objects, along with methods to add and remove them. Grails' dynamic scaffolding will automatically pick up this change and modify our views. To demonstrate this, let's add some more bootstrap code. Open TekDays/grails-app/conf/BootStrap.groovy, and add the following code to the bottom of the init block:

model/TekDays/grails-app/conf/BootStrap.groovy

```
def g1 = TekEvent.findByName('Gateway Code Camp')
g1.addToVolunteers(new TekUser(fullName: 'Sarah Martin',
                              userName: 'sarah',
                              password: '54321',
                              email: 'sarah@martinworld.com',
                              website: 'www.martinworld.com',
                              bio: 'Web designer and Grails afficianado.'))
g1.addToVolunteers(new TekUser(fullName: 'Bill Smith',
                              userName: 'Mr_Bill',
                              password: '12345',
                              email: 'mrbill@email.com',
                              website: 'www.mrbillswebsite.com',
                              bio: 'Software developer, claymation artist.'))

g1.save()
```

With this code, we retrieve a TekEvent by calling TekEvent.findByName(). Then we add new TekUser instances with the TekEvent.addToVolunteers() method, which Grails dynamically synthesizes for us. Finally, we save our TekEvent, which also saves its TekUser instances.

When we navigate to the show view for this event, we see that it contains a list of volunteer's names. Each name links to the TekUser show view for that user. (See Figure 4.3, on the following page.)

Grails also supports bidirectional one-to-many relationships with cascading deletes using the static belongsTo[2] property, which is declared in the child class, like so:

```
class Parent {
   ...
   static hasMany = [children:Child]
}

class Child {
   ...
   Parent parent
   static belongsTo = Parent
}
```

---

2. belongsTo is used to show that another class is the *owning* side of a relationship. It is used for one-to-many and many-to-many relationships.

Figure 4.3: TekEvent SHOW VIEW WITH VOLUNTEERS

4.4 Collections of Simple Data Types

We've added an organizer and a collection of volunteers to our TekEvent. That takes care of three more features from our list. We have some time left in this iteration, so let's take on another feature. We'll add the ability for anonymous users to register interest in an event.

On second thought, a completely anonymous show of interest isn't very valuable. Let's say that a person can show an interest by registering to be notified when there are updates to the event. It will still be *somewhat* anonymous, in that the user has to give only an email address. From an application viewpoint, this is also simpler; we won't have to create another domain class to represent this information. For the end user, we'll try to make it as simple as subscribing to a mailing list.

Grails provides a great way for us to associate these addresses with a TekEvent: we can use the hasMany property with a simple data type instead of a domain class. We already used hasMany to set up a collection of TekUser instances named volunteers. This time we will be setting up a String collection containing email addresses.

We need to give a meaningful name to the collection of email addresses. I think emails is a bit too generic. Sure, these are email addresses, but they represent individuals who have responded to let us know they are interested in an event. We'll go with respondents.

Let's make it so, as they say. Modify the hasMany property in TekDays/grails-app/domain/TekEvent.groovy to look like this:

```
static hasMany = [volunteers:TekUser, respondents:String]
```

With this code in place, our TekEvent now has a collection of respondents' email addresses. This change will be reflected in our scaffolded views, but that will be easier to see with some data in place. Open TekDays/grails-app/conf/BootStrap.groovy, and add a few calls to TekEvent.() addToRespondents(). It should look something like this:

```
model.1/TekDays/grails-app/conf/BootStrap.groovy
g1.addToVolunteers(new TekUser(fullName: 'Bill Smith',
                               userName: 'Mr_Bill',
                               password: '12345',
                               email: 'mrbill@email.com',
                               website: 'www.mrbillswebsite.com',
                               bio: 'Software developer and claymation artist.'))


g1.addToRespondents('ben@grailsmail.com')
g1.addToRespondents('zachary@linuxgurus.org')
g1.addToRespondents('solomon@bootstrapwelding.com')

g1.save()
```

This code is similar to the call to TekEvent.addToVolunteers() also shown here. The difference is that we are not creating new domain class instances to pass into the method—we are passing Strings instead. In Figure 4.4, on the next page, we see how the scaffolding automatically picks up this new relationship and displays it in a reasonable manner. (It's reasonable but not very fashionable. Remember we are focusing on functionality now. We'll spruce it up a bit later.)

Figure 4.4: TekEvent SHOW VIEW WITH RESPONDENTS

4.5 Adding a Sponsor Class

TekDays is geared toward community-driven technical conferences, and one of the keys to a successful community-driven conference is low cost to attendees. This can be difficult to accomplish, considering the cost of meeting space, A/V rental, food, and so on. One way to have all these necessities and still keep the registration fees low is to involve *sponsors*; in other words, companies involved in the technology or technologies featured are often willing to contribute toward the cost of the conference in exchange for a bit of exposure.

It sounds like it's time for a new domain class. We'll call our new class Sponsor. (See Figure 4.5, on the facing page.) From our project's root directory, run the following:

```
$ grails create-domain-class Sponsor
```

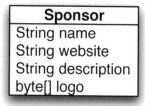

Figure 4.5: THE SPONSOR CLASS

Open the newly created TekDays/grails-app/domain/Sponsor.groovy. Enter the following code:

```
model.2/TekDays/grails-app/domain/Sponsor.groovy
class Sponsor {
    String name
    String website
    String description
    byte[] logo

    String toString(){
        name
    }

    static constraints = {
        name(blank:false)
        website(blank:false)
        description(nullable:true, maxSize:5000)
        logo(nullable:true, maxSize:1000000)
    }
}
```

There are two new things to point out in this code, both having to do with the logo property. The first is the type: byte(). The logo property will hold an image of the sponsor's logo, which will be stored as an array of bytes. The second is the constraint for logo. We added a maxSize constraint to this property in order to let the database know to use a BLOB (or other appropriate data type). Without this, many database systems would produce a field that wouldn't hold anything bigger than an icon.

We also need to create a controller to enable dynamic scaffolding. We'll do this exactly as we did for TekEvent and TekUser, but for a refresher, here it is:

```
$ grails create-controller Sponsor
```

Next, open the generated controller TekDays/grails-app/controllers/Sponsor-Controller.groovy, and modify it like so:

```
model.2/TekDays/grails-app/controllers/SponsorController.groovy
class SponsorController {

    def scaffold = Sponsor
}
```

When we run TekDays now, we see a new SponsorController link. Follow that link to the empty list view, and then click New Sponsor to open the create view. In Figure 4.6, on the next page, we see that the logo property is rendered as a *file input* element. But Grails goes beyond that: full file upload functionality is baked right in. When we save a new Sponsor, the file we've chosen for the logo will automatically be uploaded and stored in the database. After we save, we can see that the show view doesn't look that great, but we'll work on that later.

4.6 Many-to-Many Relationships

One of the concerns about bringing in a sponsor for a technical event is that the whole thing might turn into a commercial for a vendor. That becomes much less of a concern if there are multiple sponsors for an event. On the other hand, a single company might be interested in sponsoring more than one event. So, should a TekEvent have a collection of Sponsor instances, or should Sponsor have a collection of TekEvent instances? The short answer is *both*. The longer answer, which we'll get to shortly, is *neither*.

The relationship between TekEvent and Sponsor is a *many-to-many* relationship. Grails supports many-to-many relationships implicitly by having each class include the other in its hasMany block. In this arrangement, each class will have a collection of the other, but one side has to be declared as the owning side. For this, Grails uses the static variable belongsTo.

Figure 4.6: Sponsor create view

Here's an example:

```
class TekEvent {
  ...
  static hasMany=[..., sponsors:Sponsor]
}

class Sponsor {
  ...
  static hasMany=[events:TekEvent]
  static belongsTo=TekEvent
}
```

This code would create the relationships, or links, between a TekEvent and its collection of Sponsor instances, as well as between a Sponsor and its collection of TekEvent instances. What it wouldn't do is tell us anything about the *relationship* itself. When our users are organizing an event, it's great that they're able to see who their sponsors are, but it would also be helpful to know *what* each sponsor is contributing.

Figure 4.7: THE SPONSORSHIP CLASS

Are they providing the meeting space, A/V equipment, food, T-shirts (a critical piece of a successful event), or a cash contribution? If they are contributing cash, how much?

To store this type of information, we will need an intermediary class. We'll call this class Sponsorship. (See Figure 4.7.) This class will have a reference to a single TekEvent and a single Sponsor, with fields to tell us more about what the sponsor is providing for the event. Let's go ahead and create this class:

```
$ grails create-domain-class Sponsorship
```

We'll implement this class with the following code:

model.3/TekDays/grails-app/domain/Sponsorship.groovy

```
class Sponsorship {
    TekEvent event
    Sponsor sponsor
    String contributionType
    String description
    String notes

    static constraints = {
        event(nullable:false)
        sponsor(nullable:false)
        contributionType(inList:["Other", "Venue", "A/V", "Promotion", "Cash"])
        description(nullable:true, blank:true)
        notes(nullable:true, blank:true, maxSize:5000)
    }
}
```

In this class, we're using a new constraint. The inList constraint takes as its value a list of Strings. Only values matching one of the items in the list will be allowed; any other values will cause a constraint violation when saving. But wait, there's more. Grails will also use this constraint to render an HTML <select> element in the scaffolded views. We'll take a look at that shortly, but first we have a little more plumbing to do.

We need to modify TekEvent and Sponsor so that they each have a collection of Sponsorship instances. Open TekDays/grails-app/domain/Sponsor. groovy, and add a hasMany property. Then add a new constraint to the constraint block, like so:

model.3/TekDays/grails-app/domain/Sponsor.groovy

```
static hasMany=[sponsorships:Sponsorship]

static constraints = {
    name(blank:false)
    website(blank:false)
    description(nullable:true, maxSize:5000)
    logo(nullable:true, maxSize:1000000)
    sponsorships(nullable:true)
}
```

Repeat those steps with TekDays/grails-app/domain/TekEvent.groovy:

model.2/TekDays/grails-app/domain/TekEvent.groovy

```
    static hasMany = [volunteers:TekUser,
                      respondents:String,
                      sponsorships:Sponsorship]

    static constraints = {
        name()
        city()
        description(maxSize : 5000)
        organizer()
        venue()
        startDate()
        endDate()
        volunteers(nullable : true)
        sponsorships(nullable : true)
    }
```

One last step: let's add some sponsorship data in our BootStrap so that we'll have something to look at. Open TekDays/grails-app/conf/BootStrap. groovy, and add the following code to the bottom of the init block:

model.2/TekDays/grails-app/conf/BootStrap.groovy

```
def s1 = new Sponsor(name:'Contegix',
                     website:'contegix.com',
                     description:'Beyond Managed Hosting for your Enterprise'
                        ).save()
def s2 = new Sponsor(name:'Object Computing Incorporated',
                     website:'ociweb.com',
                     description:'An OO Software Engineering Company'
                        ).save()
def sp1 = new Sponsorship(event:g1,
                          sponsor:s1,
                          contributionType:'Other',
                          description:'Cool T-Shirts')
```

Figure 4.8: TEKEVENT SHOW VIEW WITH SPONSORSHIPS

```
def sp2 = new Sponsorship(event:g1,
                          sponsor:s2,
                          contributionType:'Venue',
                          description:'Will be paying for the Moscone')
s1.addToSponsorships(sp1)
s1.save()
s2.addToSponsorships(sp2)
s2.save()
g1.addToSponsorships(sp1)
g1.addToSponsorships(sp2)
g1.save()
```

When we run the application and navigate to the TekEvent show view, we see something like Figure 4.8. Notice that the Sponsorship instances are shown as *Sponsorship:1*. This is because we did not define a toString() for the Sponsorship class. If you're following along (and I do hope you are), you may also notice that clicking the Sponsorship link leads to an error page. This is because we haven't created a SponsorshipController

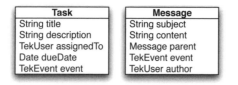

Figure 4.9: THE TASK AND MESSAGE CLASSES

to enable the scaffolding. We'll be addressing this soon. Also, as we go about cleaning up our user interface, we'll have different ways to display a Sponsorship, depending on the context; but for now, this serves to show us that the one-to-many relationship is established correctly. Well done!

4.7 Finishing Up the Domain Model

Looking again at our feature list, we can see that we'll need two more domain classes. We're going to have a list of *tasks* that need to be done to prepare for an event. That will require a Task class. We're also going to have a simple forum that the organizer and volunteers can use to communicate throughout the process. For this, we will need a Message class. For a view of these classes, see Figure 4.9.

We'll create the Task class first. Run grails create-domain-class Task, and add the following code to TekDays/grails-app/domain/Task.groovy:

`model.2/TekDays/grails-app/domain/Task.groovy`

```
class Task {
    String title
    String notes
    TekUser assignedTo
    Date dueDate
    TekEvent event

    static constraints = {
        title(blank:false)
        notes(blank:true, nullable:true, maxSize:5000)
        assignedTo(nullable:true)
        dueDate(nullable:true)
    }

    static belongsTo = TekEvent
}
```

Next we'll create the Message class and add the following code to TekDays/grails-app/domain/Message.groovy:

model.2/TekDays/grails-app/domain/Message.groovy

```
class Message {
    String subject
    String content
    Message parent
    TekEvent event
    TekUser author

    static constraints = {
        subject(blank:false)
        content(blank:false, maxSize:2000)
        parent(nullable:true)
        author(nullable:false)
    }

    static belongsTo = TekEvent
}
```

There's not much to look at in these classes other than the belongsTo. You'll notice that both of these classes have the following line: belongsTo = TekEvent. This is because these classes will be involved in bidirectional one-to-many relationships with the TekEvent class and we want cascading deletes. For example, we know that a Message will belong to only one TekEvent, and if that TekEvent goes away, there is no reason to keep the Message. To complete these relationships, we will need to once again modify our TekEvent. We'll modify the hasMany property and add two more constraints to TekDays/grails-app/domain/TekEvent.groovy. Note the highlighted lines.

Since we've made so many changes to this class, we'll show the whole thing here for the sake of clarity:

model.3/TekDays/grails-app/domain/TekEvent.groovy

```
class TekEvent {
    String city
    String name
    TekUser organizer
    String venue
    Date startDate
    Date endDate
    String description

    String toString(){
        "$name, $city"
    }
```

```
    static hasMany = [volunteers:TekUser,
                      respondents:String,
                      sponsorships:Sponsorship,
▶                    tasks:Task,
▶                    messages:Message]

    static constraints = {
        name()
        city()
        description(maxSize : 5000)
        organizer()
        venue()
        startDate()
        endDate()
        volunteers(nullable : true)
        sponsorships(nullable : true)
▶       tasks(nullable : true)
▶       messages(nullable : true)
    }
}
```

4.8 Summary

In this iteration, we created our domain model, defined and discussed the relationships between various classes in our model, and set up bootstrap data that we can use to bring our model to life during development.

Now that we have our domain model set up the way we want, we are ready to generate the code that will enable us to make more significant changes in our application. In the next chapter, we'll generate and review the code behind all of the functionality we've seen so far.

Constraints and Validation

Constraints are used in generating scaffolded views for a domain class as well as for hints in generating the database schema. But the real power of constraints is the part they play in validation. When we call save() or validate() on one of our domain class instances, Grails will try to validate the instance against any constraints we have assigned. If any of the constraints are not met, the save() or validate() call will fail, and appropriate error information will be stored in the instance's errors* property.

Grails provides several handy constraints that we can take advantage of, but it also gives us the ability to define custom constraints, so the possibilities are endless. Here are some of the more useful built-in constraints:

- blank (true/false): Allows an empty string value.
- nullable (true/false): Allows null values.
- max: Maximum value.
- min: Minimum value.
- vsize: Takes a Groovy range to determine bounds.
- maxSize: The maximum size of a String or Collection.
- minSize: The minimum size of a String or Collection.
- inList: Value must be included in the supplied listv
- matches: Value must match a regular expression.
- unique (true/false): Enforces uniqueness in the database.
- url (true/false): Value must be a valid URL.
- email (true/false): Value must be a valid email address.
- creditCard (true/false): Value must be a valid credit card number.
- validator: Takes a closure for custom validation. The first parameter is the value, and the second (optional) parameter is the instance being validated.

---

*. Error details can be found by calling errors.allErrors.each{//iterate over errors}.

Chapter 5

Beyond Scaffolding

So far, our TekDays application contains six persistent domain classes, three controllers, and twelve views—and all with less than 130 lines of code. Now, Grails uses the Groovy programming language, and Groovy is known for its conciseness, but even in Groovy, this much functionality takes more than 130 lines of code. In fact, it's Grails' dynamic scaffolding that is creating all this for us at runtime. Scaffolding is a great feature; we've been taking advantage of it to gradually build and tweak our domain model, and all the while we've been able to see the effects in our views. However, it's time to remove the training wheels and start taking control of our code.

5.1 Generating Scaffolding Code

Grails gives us an easy way to generate the code that does what the dynamic scaffolding has been doing for us. We won't see any changes to the application, but we will have the code necessary to make changes. To get started, we will use the grails generate-all script.

The generate-all script can be called in a few different ways. If you call it with no arguments, you will be prompted for a name. (By convention, this would be a domain class name.) For the more argumentative types, you can call generate-all with a name as the argument. Both of these approaches generate a controller and four views (.gsp files). This second method is what I usually use after creating a new domain class, but since we have several domain classes for which we want to generate corresponding controllers and views, we will use a third option. Sometimes referred to as *uber-generate-all*, this modification to the generate-all script was contributed by Marcel Overdijk.[1] Let's try it:

```
$ grails generate-all "*"
```

Once this script gets going, it will prompt you to confirm the replacement of the controllers that we created earlier. Go ahead and let them be replaced. We won't need the old ones anymore. When it's done, you'll see the statement Finished generation for domain classes.

If we run the application now, we will have all the features that we had before we generated the code and then some. You may recall that we created controllers and enabled dynamic scaffolding for only three of our domain classes (TekEvent, TekUser, and Sponsor). We now have controllers for Sponsorship, Task, and Message. We may not end up keeping all of this generated code, but it makes a great learning tool, and these files can serve as stubs to which we can add custom code. Let's take a closer look at the code we've generated.

5.2 Anatomy of a Grails Controller

Let's examine the TekEventController first: what is it doing for us, and what else we can do with it? Open TekDays/grails-app/controllers/TekEventController.groovy, and follow along as we take a look at it in chunks:

beyond/TekDays/grails-app/controllers/TekEventController.groovy
```
class TekEventController {

    def index = { redirect(action:list,params:params) }

    // the delete, save and update actions only accept POST requests
    static allowedMethods = [delete:'POST', save:'POST', update:'POST']

    def list = {
        params.max = Math.min( params.max ? params.max.toInteger() : 10,  100)
        [ tekEventInstanceList: TekEvent.list( params ),
          tekEventInstanceTotal: TekEvent.count() ]
    }
```

The first thing we see is the *class declaration*. A Grails controller is a plain Groovy class. There is nothing to extend, and there are no interfaces to implement. Controllers serve as the entry points into a Grails application.

---

1. http://marceloverdijk.blogspot.com/

The work done by a controller is done in an *action*. Actions are closure properties of the controller.[2] Every closure declared in a controller is an action and can be accessed via a URL in the pattern: /app-name/controllerBaseName/action. The first letter of the controller's name will be lowercased, and the word *Controller* will be left off.

There are three options to properly exit a controller action. We can call the render() method, which is added to all controllers and takes the name of a *view* along with a Map containing any data the view needs. We can call the redirect() method (which is also added to all controllers) to issue an HTTP redirect to another URL. (We'll look at this method more closely in the next section.) And we can return *null*, or a Map containing data, which is referred to as a *model*. In this last case, Grails will attempt to render a view with the same name as the action. It will look for this view in a directory named after the root name of the controller; for example, returning from the list action of the TekEventController will cause Grails to render the view /grails-app/views/tekEvent/list.gsp.

The Index Action

The index action is the default action that is called when we navigate to this controller. For example, if we follow the link on the default home page for the TekEventController, we'll be calling http://localhost:8080/TekDays/tekEvent. This will call the index action. By default, this action just redirects to the list action using the redirect() method we mentioned earlier. The redirect() method takes a Map as a parameter; this allows it to take several optional parameters as entries in the Map. The ones we'll use most often are controller, action, and params. (If the controller is not specified, the current controller will be used, and if the action is not specified, the index action will be used.) The params is also a Map, which holds any request parameters. The redirect() method issues an HTTP redirect to a URL constructed from these parameters.

The List Action

The first line of the list closure is working with the params property, which, as we saw earlier, is a Map containing all the parameters of the incoming request. Since it is a Groovy Map, any element to which we assign a value will be added if it doesn't exist.

---

2. One nice thing about actions being closures is that we can safely declare methods in a controller without worrying about them also being accessible via a URL.

Take a look at the following line:

```
params.max = Math.min( params.max ? params.max.toInteger() : 10,  100)
```

In this code, we see the max element being added to the params. The value that is being set is the return value of the Math.min() method. Math.min() is being passed the existing max value, if there is one, or the default of 10, along with the constant of 100. This is just a bit of protection that Grails gives us against trying to pull too many items at once. If we tried to access this view with http://localhost:8080/TekDays/tekEvent/list?max=1000, we would get only 100 results (assuming we had that many events entered—why not think big?).

The last two lines make up a single statement that declares and returns a Map with two elements: tekEventInstanceList and tekEventInstanceTotal. The tekEventInstanceList is being loaded with a call to TekEvent.list().[3] The list() is being passed the params map, from which it will pull any parameters that it can use.[4] The tekEventInstanceTotal is loaded with TekEvent.count(). This value will be used in the pagination built into the list view, which we will look at shortly.

The end result of the list action is that the list view is rendered using the data in the Map that's returned from this action. This is done using the conventions we discussed earlier. It's important to note that this feature is not limited to the generated actions and views. As we'll see in Chapter 9, *Big-Picture Views*, on page 141, we can create custom actions and views, and if we follow the conventions, it will just work!

The Show Action

The show action expects an id parameter. Since many of the scaffolded actions expect an id parameter, Grails provides a URL mapping that enables the id to be part of the URL.[5] If we navigate to the show view of one of our events, our browser address bar will show something like this: http://localhost:8080/TekDays/tekEvent/show/1.

---

3. list() is one of the dynamic methods added to our domain classes. See Section 3.2, *More About Domain Classes*, on page 29.
4. This brings up another powerful feature of Grails. Many methods in Grails take a Map as a parameter. These methods will look in the Map for the elements they need and ignore the rest. That means that in one action we can pass the params Map to several different methods, and each will just take from it what it needs. Pretty cool, huh?
5. We'll discuss URL mapping in Section 11.4, *User-Friendly URLs*, on page 190.

beyond/TekDays/grails-app/controllers/TekEventController.groovy

```
def show = {
    def tekEventInstance = TekEvent.get( params.id )

    if(!tekEventInstance) {
        flash.message = "TekEvent not found with id ${params.id}"
        redirect(action:list)
    }
    else { return [ tekEventInstance : tekEventInstance ] }
}
```

The first line of the show action calls the TekEvent.get() method to retrieve the TekEvent referred to by the id parameter. Then there is some nifty built-in error checking.

If no domain class instance exists with the id passed in, an error message is stored in the flash Map, and the user is redirected to the list view.[6] This gets even better, as we will soon see, in that the list view is already set up to display this message.

If a TekEvent instance is found with the id passed in, it is returned in a Map with the **key** of tekEventInstance. Finally, the show action will render the show view.

The Delete Action

The delete action is available, by default, in the edit and show views. It must be called via a POST method. Going back to the beginning of our TekEventController listing, we see the allowedMethods property. This is a Map containing actions and the HTTP methods that can be used to call them. This prevents a user from entering something like http://localhost:8080/TekDays/tekEvent/delete/1 and deleting our event.

beyond/TekDays/grails-app/controllers/TekEventController.groovy

```
def delete = {
    def tekEventInstance = TekEvent.get( params.id )
    if(tekEventInstance) {
        try {
            tekEventInstance.delete()
            flash.message = "TekEvent ${params.id} deleted"
            redirect(action:list)
        }
```

---

6. flash is often referred to as a *scope*. I think it's more accurate to refer to it as a Map that exists in a special scope. Values stored in flash are available for this request and one following request, which allows us to store a message before redirecting and have that message be available to the redirected view.

```
            catch(org.springframework.dao.DataIntegrityViolationException e) {
                flash.message = "TekEvent ${params.id} could not be deleted"
                redirect(action:show,id:params.id)
            }
        }
        else {
            flash.message = "TekEvent not found with id ${params.id}"
            redirect(action:list)
        }
    }
```

The delete action starts out much like the show action. It attempts to retrieve a TekEvent instance and redirects to the list view if it can't find one. That's where the similarities end.

If an instance is found, we enter a **try/catch** block, where we try to delete the instance. If the deletion is successful, we store a message in flash and redirect to the list view. If there is an exception, we store a different message in flash and redirect to the show view. There is no delete view, for obvious reasons.

The Edit Action

beyond/TekDays/grails-app/controllers/TekEventController.groovy

```
def edit = {
    def tekEventInstance = TekEvent.get( params.id )

    if(!tekEventInstance) {
        flash.message = "TekEvent not found with id ${params.id}"
        redirect(action:list)
    }
    else {
        return [ tekEventInstance : tekEventInstance ]
    }
}
```

The edit action doesn't do any editing itself: that's left up to the update action. Instead, edit loads up the necessary data and passes it to the edit view. Except for the name (which determines the view rendered), the edit action is identical to the show action.

The Update Action

The update action steps up to bat when changes from the edit view are submitted.

```groovy
def update = {
    def tekEventInstance = TekEvent.get( params.id )
    if(tekEventInstance) {
        if(params.version) {
            def version = params.version.toLong()
            if(tekEventInstance.version > version) {

                tekEventInstance.errors.rejectValue("version",
                    "tekEvent.optimistic.locking.failure",
                    "Another user has updated this TekEvent " +
                        "while you were editing.")
                render(view:'edit',model:[tekEventInstance:tekEventInstance])
                return
            }
        }
        tekEventInstance.properties = params
        if(!tekEventInstance.hasErrors() && tekEventInstance.save()) {
            flash.message = "TekEvent ${params.id} updated"
            redirect(action:show,id:tekEventInstance.id)
        }
        else {
            render(view:'edit',model:[tekEventInstance:tekEventInstance])
        }
    }
    else {
        flash.message = "TekEvent not found with id ${params.id}"
        redirect(action:edit,id:params.id)
    }
}
```

Like earlier actions, update tries to retrieve a TekEvent instance with the id parameter. In this case, the id will be coming from a hidden field in the edit view. If an instance is found, we perform some *optimistic concurrency* checking.[7] If all that goes well, we come to a very interesting step.

With a single line, we will assign all the values from the edit view to the appropriate property of the TekEvent instance, including any necessary data conversion!

```groovy
tekEventInstance.properties = params
```

This is Grails data binding in action, and it's a beautiful thing. Just think of how many lines of code that would take in most other web development tools. You gotta love it!

---

7. See http://en.wikipedia.org/wiki/Optimistic_concurrency_control.

Once all the incoming values have been set, we check to make sure the instance is valid and if it can be saved to the database. If both of those steps are successful, we receive a "success" message in flash and are directed to the show view. If either step fails, a "failure" message is stored in flash, and we get directed back to the edit view.

The Create Action

`beyond/TekDays/grails-app/controllers/TekEventController.groovy`

```groovy
def create = {
    def tekEventInstance = new TekEvent()
    tekEventInstance.properties = params
    return ['tekEventInstance':tekEventInstance]
}
```

The create action creates a new TekEvent instance and then assigns the params to its properties property. (We'll see why this is done shortly.) Then it returns that instance in a Map with the key of tekEventInstance. Finally, it renders the create view.

The Save Action

`beyond/TekDays/grails-app/controllers/TekEventController.groovy`

```groovy
    def save = {
        def tekEventInstance = new TekEvent(params)
        if(!tekEventInstance.hasErrors() && tekEventInstance.save()) {
            flash.message = "TekEvent ${tekEventInstance.id} created"
            redirect(action:show,id:tekEventInstance.id)
        }
        else {
            render(view:'create',model:[tekEventInstance:tekEventInstance])
        }
    }
}
```

The save action is called from the create view. It correlates to the update action and does pretty much the same thing, minus the concurrency check (which isn't an issue when creating new records). If all is well, the show view is rendered with the newly created instance. If there are problems, the user is redirected to the create action. (This is why the params are assigned to the tekEventInstance.properties in the create action.)

So, that's a tour of the generated actions of a Grails controller. We looked at only one of the six controllers generated by the generate-all script, but they all have the same code with different domain classes.

Feel free to browse the rest of them. It should all look very familiar. Now we'll see what Grails gives us for views.

5.3 Grails Views with Groovy Server Pages

Grails uses Groovy Server Pages (GSP) for its view layer. If you've ever worked with JavaServer Pages, well, you have my sympathy, but GSP will seem familiar—only easier to work with. Grails also uses SiteMesh,[8] the page decoration framework from OpenSymphony, to assist in the page layout. SiteMesh will merge each of our .gsp files into a file called main.gsp. This is what gives a consistent look to all of our pages, as we saw with the dynamic scaffolding. We'll begin our tour of the generated views with main.gsp, followed by the four views generated for the TekEvent class. Then we'll look at a couple of the other views that take advantage of additional Grails features.

Exploring main.gsp

`beyond/TekDays/grails-app/views/layouts/main.gsp`

```
<html>
  <head>
    <title><g:layoutTitle default="Grails" /></title>
    <link rel="stylesheet"
          href="${resource(dir:'css',file:'main.css')}" />
    <link rel="shortcut icon"
          href="${resource(dir:'images',file:'favicon.ico')}"
          type="image/x-icon" />
    <g:layoutHead />
    <g:javascript library="application" />
  </head>
  <body>
    <div id="spinner" class="spinner" style="display:none;">
      <img src="${resource(dir:'images',file:'spinner.gif')}" alt="Spinner"/>
    </div>
    <div class="logo">
      <img src="${resource(dir:'images',file:'grails_logo.jpg')}" alt="Grails"/>
    </div>
    <g:layoutBody />
  </body>
</html>
```

main.gsp starts out with a *<title>* in the *<head>* section. This tag contains a *<g:layoutTitle>* tag, which will substitute the *<title>* from the

---

8. http://opensymphony.com/sitemesh

Figure 5.1: TEKEVENT LIST VIEW

view that is being merged. Next, it links in a style sheet and favicon[9] that will be used by all views. Then there is the *<g:layoutHead>* tag. This will merge in the contents of the target view's *<head>* section. The *<body>* section contains a spinner image, an application logo, and a *<g:layoutBody>* tag, which merges in the *<body>* contents of the target view.

As you can see, this file gives us a convenient place to make some major improvements to our application. And that's just what we're going to do, as soon as we finish our tour. As we discuss the four generated views, we will be looking at only portions of them, for the sake of space. I'll give you the name and path for each file so you can open each one on your system and follow along.

The List View

The TekEvent list view is shown in Figure 5.1. You can refer to that image as we look at the GSP code behind it. You'll find this code in TekDays/grails-app/views/tekEvent/list.gsp.

---

9. http://en.wikipedia.org/wiki/Favicon

```
<span class="menuButton">
  <a class="home" href="${resource(dir:'')}">Home</a>
</span>
<span class="menuButton">
  <g:link class="create" action="create">New TekEvent</g:link>
</span>
```

This code creates the button bar just below the Grails logo. We can see two ways that Grails provides for creating links. The resource() method takes a relative path and creates a URL, which is assigned to the href attribute of an anchor tag. The <g:link> tag creates an anchor tag using the values of the controller, action, and id attributes (if they're provided). If a controller is not provided, the current controller is assumed. In this case, a link to the create action of the TekEventController will be created.

```
<g:if test="${flash.message}">
  <div class="message">${flash.message}</div>
</g:if>
```

This code doesn't show up in Figure 5.1, on the preceding page, but it is important to take note of. Recall that during our discussion of controllers, we often had code that would store text in the message element of flash. This is where that text will show up. The <g:if> tag checks for the existence of flash.message and, if found, displays it.

```
<g:sortableColumn property="name" title="Name" />
<g:sortableColumn property="city" title="City" />
<g:sortableColumn property="description" title="Description" />
<th>Organizer</th>
<g:sortableColumn property="venue" title="Venue" />
```

The <g:sortableColumn> tag is what Grails uses to provide sorting on our list view. Note that, by default, this works only with regular properties, not object references or collections. That is why we see a <th> tag used for the organizer property.

```
<g:each in="${tekEventInstanceList}" status="i"
                              var="tekEventInstance">
  <tr class="${(i % 2) == 0 ? 'odd' : 'even'}">
    <td>
      <g:link action="show" id="${tekEventInstance.id}">
        ${fieldValue(bean:tekEventInstance, field:'id')}
      </g:link></td>
    <td>${fieldValue(bean:tekEventInstance, field:'name')}</td>
    <td>${fieldValue(bean:tekEventInstance, field:'city')}</td>
    <td>${fieldValue(bean:tekEventInstance, field:'description')}</td>
    <td>${fieldValue(bean:tekEventInstance, field:'organizer')}</td>
    <td>${fieldValue(bean:tekEventInstance, field:'venue')}</td>
  </tr>
</g:each>
```

This code is the heart of the list view. We start with the *<g:each>* tag, which iterates over the list that we passed in from the controller. Each item in the list is assigned to the tekEventInstance variable. The body of the *<g:each>* tag fills in the table row with the properties of the tekEventInstance. Notice that a Groovy expression is used to determine the CSS class of the *<tr>*—powerful stuff! Inside the *<td>* tags, the fieldValue() method is used to render the value of each TekEvent property. We'll learn more about the fieldValue() method when we look at the create view.

```
<div class="paginateButtons">
  <g:paginate total="${tekEventInstanceTotal}" />
</div>
```

The final portion of the list.gsp we'll look at is another one that we can't see in Figure 5.1, on page 76. The *<g:paginate>* tag would cause pagination buttons to show up at the bottom of the list view if we had enough events displayed to warrant it. This tag uses the total that we passed in from the controller's list action.

The Show View

The show view, pictured in Figure 5.2, on the next page, is in TekDays/ grails-app/views/tekEvent/show.gsp. Open this file now as we look at a few interesting sections:

```
<tr class="prop">
  <td valign="top" class="name">Id:</td>
  <td valign="top" class="value">
    ${fieldValue(bean:tekEventInstance, field:'id')}
  </td>
</tr>
<tr class="prop">
  <td valign="top" class="name">Name:</td>
  <td valign="top" class="value">
    ${fieldValue(bean:tekEventInstance, field:'name')}
  </td>
</tr>
```

This code shows a couple of examples of how Grails displays text properties. Notice the CSS class hierarchy. The *<tr>* tag has a prop class, and the *<td>* tags can have a name or value class.

Figure 5.2: TEKEVENT SHOW VIEW

```
<tr class="prop">
  <td valign="top" class="name">Organizer:</td>
  <td valign="top" class="value">
    <g:link controller="tekUser" action="show"
            id="${tekEventInstance?.organizer?.id}">
      ${tekEventInstance?.organizer?.encodeAsHTML()}
    </g:link>
  </td>
</tr>
```

Here we have an example of the way Grails displays a related object. The organizer property is rendered as a link to the TekUser show view. The <g:link> tag has its controller and action attributes set accordingly. The id is set to a Groovy expression that reads the id property of the organizer property of the tekEventInstance that we passed in from the controller. Notice the ? after the tekEventInstance and organizer references; this is

Groovy's *safe navigation* operator. When this expression is evaluated, if either of these items is null, the whole expression evaluates to null, and no exception is thrown. This operator has saved the world from untold numbers of if blocks!

```
<tr class="prop">
  <td valign="top" class="name">Start Date:</td>
  <td valign="top" class="value">
    ${fieldValue(bean:tekEventInstance, field:'startDate')}
  </td>
</tr>
```

The startDate is a Date type, and yet it is rendered the same way as a text property. Grails handles the conversion from Date to String for us.

```
<tr class="prop">
  <td valign="top" class="name">Volunteers:</td>
  <td  valign="top" style="text-align:left;" class="value">
    <ul>
      <g:each var="v" in="${tekEventInstance.volunteers}">
        <li><g:link controller="tekUser" action="show" id="${v.id}">
          ${v?.encodeAsHTML()}
        </g:link></li>
      </g:each>
    </ul>
  </td>
</tr>
```

The Grails scaffolding renders one-to-many relationships as an unordered list. Here we see the volunteers property being displayed using a *<g:each>* tag inside a *<ul>* tag. Another thing to notice here is the use of the encodeAsHTML() method. This method is added to all String objects and prevents any HTML code from being processed while the page is rendering. This is helpful in defending against cross-site scripting attacks.[10]

```
<tr class="prop">
  <td valign="top" class="name">Respondents:</td>
  <td valign="top" class="value">
    ${fieldValue(bean:tekEventInstance, field:'respondents')}
  </td>
</tr>
```

Rounding out the show view, we have the respondents collection. This property is a collection of String objects containing email addresses. This type of collection is rendered as if it were a single String field.

---

10. http://en.wikipedia.org/wiki/Cross-site_scripting

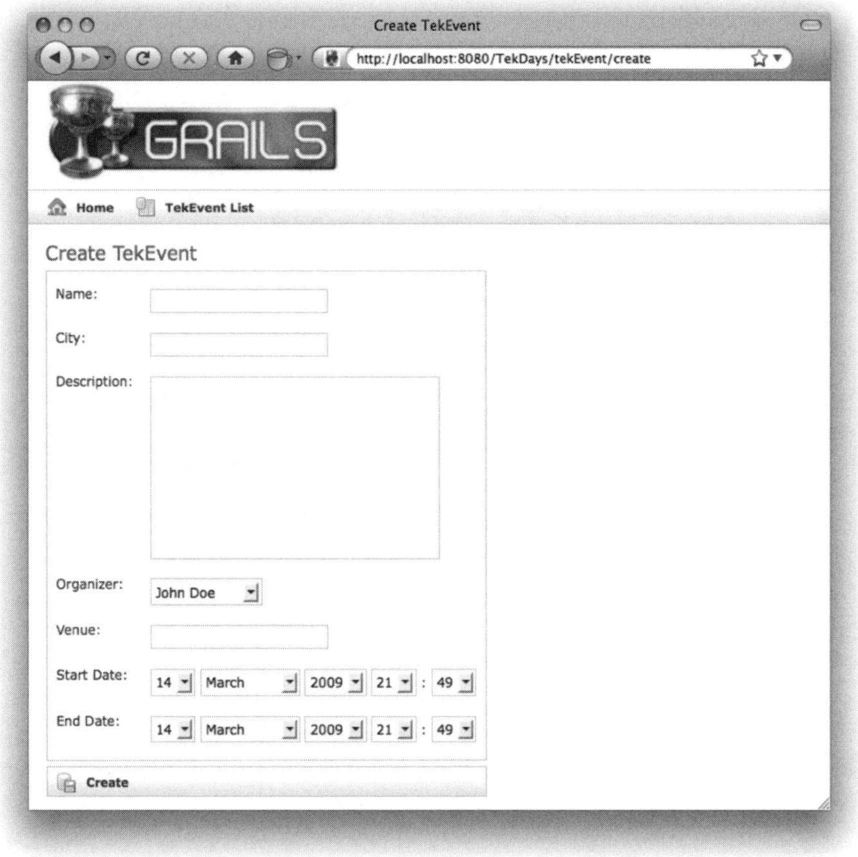

Figure 5.3: TekEvent CREATE VIEW

Grails handles converting it to a comma-separated list, as we can see in Figure 5.2, on page 79. If we wanted to, we could use a *<g:each>* tag to show these as a list or in a table.

The Create View

We can see the create view in Figure 5.3. The code for this view is in TekDays/grails-app/views/tekEvent/create.gsp. Open this file, and we'll see what new and exciting things it has in store for us:

```
<g:hasErrors bean="${tekEventInstance}">
  <div class="errors">
    <g:renderErrors bean="${tekEventInstance}" as="list" />
  </div>
</g:hasErrors>
```

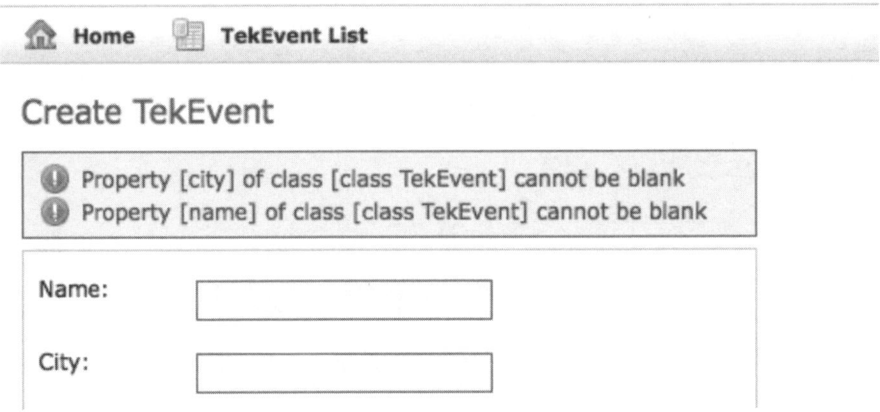

🏠 **Home**   📋 **TekEvent List**

Create TekEvent

> ⓘ Property [city] of class [class TekEvent] cannot be blank
> ⓘ Property [name] of class [class TekEvent] cannot be blank

Name:

City:

Figure 5.4: BUILT-IN ERROR HANDLING

In Section 5.3, *The List View*, on page 76, we saw how messages that we set in the controller are displayed in the view. Here we see another type of message block. When a domain instance fails to save, errors are stored in an errors property. The <*g:hasErrors*> tag is a conditional tag that examines the domain instance assigned to its bean attribute and renders its body if errors are found. In the body of the tag, we find the <*g:renderErrors*> tag, which will display the errors in a list at the top of the page. (See Figure 5.4.)

```
<g:form action="save" method="post" >
```

The <*g:form*> tag sets up an HTML form. This tag has controller, action, and id attributes, which will result in the URL to submit the form to. In this case, we're using only the action attribute.

```
<tr class="prop">
  <td valign="top" class="name">
    <label for="name">Name:</label>
  </td>
  <td valign="top" class="value
      ${hasErrors(bean:tekEventInstance,field:'name','errors')}">
    <input type="text"
           id="name"
           name="name"
           value="${fieldValue(bean:tekEventInstance,field:'name')}"/>
  </td>
</tr>
```

The create view uses the same two-column table layout as the show view. The difference is that here the second column contains HTML input elements. Notice how the <g:hasErrors> tag is used in a Groovy expression to determine the CSS class to use. It doesn't look like a tag, does it? All GSP tags can also be called as methods. How's that for versatile?

Next, the value attribute of the input element is set to another Groovy expression using the fieldValue() method. This is where this method really shines.

In Section 5.2, *The Save Action*, on page 74, we saw that if validation fails, we redirect the user to the create view. In this case, we don't want to show the actual values of the tekEventInstance. We want to redisplay the values that the user has entered. These values are stored as part of the errors collection, and fieldValue() knows how to get them. If there are no errors, then the tekEventInstance properties are displayed. This method also calls encodeAsHTML() for us, since that is almost always what we want.

```
<tr class="prop">
  <td valign="top" class="name">
    <label for="description">Description:</label>
  </td>
  <td valign="top" class="value
    ${hasErrors(bean:tekEventInstance,field:'description','errors')}">
    <textarea rows="5" cols="40" name="description">
      ${fieldValue(bean:tekEventInstance, field:'description')}
    </textarea>
  </td>
</tr>
```

For the description property, Grails is using a <*textarea*> element:

```
<tr class="prop">
  <td valign="top" class="name">
    <label for="startDate">Start Date:</label>
  </td>
  <td valign="top" class="value $
      {hasErrors(bean:tekEventInstance,field:'startDate','errors')}">
    <g:datePicker name="startDate"
                  value="${tekEventInstance?.startDate}" >
    </g:datePicker>
  </td>
</tr>
```

The <g:datePicker> tag renders that series of select elements that we see in Figure 5.3, on page 81. This tag can be configured to be much more useful by using the precision and noSelection attributes.[11]

The Edit View

The last of the scaffolded views is the edit view. See Figure 5.5, on the facing page. You will find the code in TekDays/grails-app/views/tekEvent/edit.gsp. By now, we've seen most areas of interest covered in the preceding views, but open this one and follow along as we see what nuggets might be awaiting discovery:

```
<tr class="prop">
  <td valign="top" class="name">
    <label for="organizer">Organizer:</label>
  </td>
  <td valign="top" class="value
      ${hasErrors(bean:tekEventInstance,field:'organizer','errors')}">
    <g:select optionKey="id" from="${TekUser.list()}"
              name="organizer.id"
              value="${tekEventInstance?.organizer?.id}" >
    </g:select>
  </td>
</tr>
```

Here's something new. For properties that are references to another domain class, Grails uses a <g:select> tag, which will render a <select> element loaded with all the available choices for that class. In this case, we end up with a list of TekUser instances that can be assigned to the organizer property.

```
<tr class="prop">
  <td valign="top" class="name">
    <label for="volunteers">Volunteers:</label>
  </td>
  <td valign="top" class="value
      ${hasErrors(bean:tekEventInstance,field:'volunteers','errors')}">
    <g:select name="volunteers" from="${TekUser.list()}"
              size="5" multiple="yes" optionKey="id"
              value="${tekEventInstance?.volunteers}" />

  </td>
</tr>
```

Grails also uses a <g:select> tag for unidirectional one-to-many relationships. In this case, the multiple attribute is set to yes, and the value

---

11. See http://www.grails.org/doc/1.1/ref/Tags/datePicker.html.

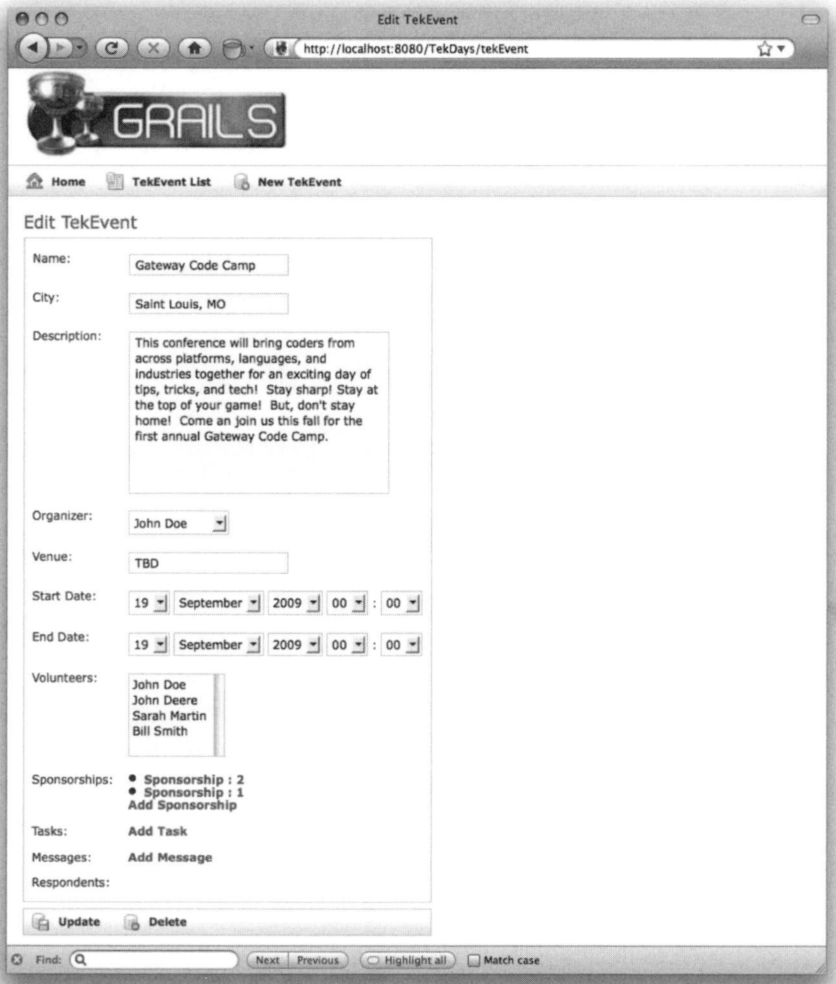

Figure 5.5: TekEvent edit view

attribute is set to the volunteers collection property. This will render a multiselect listbox loaded with TekUser instances. When submitted, all the selected instances are automagically added to the volunteers property.

```
<tr class="prop">
  <td valign="top" class="name">
    <label for="sponsorships">Sponsorships:</label>
  </td>
  <td valign="top" class="value
      ${hasErrors(bean:tekEventInstance,field:'sponsorships','errors')}">
    <ul>
      <g:each var="s" in="${tekEventInstance?.sponsorships?}">
        <li>
          <g:link controller="sponsorship" action="show"
                  id="${s.id}">${s?.encodeAsHTML()}</g:link>
        </li>
      </g:each>
    </ul>
    <g:link controller="sponsorship"
            params="['tekEvent.id':tekEventInstance?.id]"
            action="create">
    Add Sponsorship
    </g:link>
  </td>
</tr>
```

In this block, we can see how the sponsorship collection property is rendered as an unordered list of links. We already saw this in Section 5.3, *The Show View*, on page 78. What's interesting here is that immediately after the <ul> tag is closed, there is a <g:link> tag that will render a link to the create action of the SponsorshipController. The value in the params attribute will cause this TekEvent instance to be assigned to the tekEvent property of the newly created Sponsorship.

And this concludes our tour of the code behind the scaffolded views. Now that this code is available to us and we have a working understanding of what it is doing, we can see how we could make a few changes to make our application a little better looking and easier to use. We'll do that beginning in the next chapter, but first, let's see how we can hook up to a real database so we no longer lose our data changes every time we restart the application.

5.4 Configuring a Database

The in-memory database that comes with Grails is handy and we have been making good use of it, but a time comes in the life of any application when you need to have your data stored in a real database. (Let's hope this happens before you go to production.) As with most things, Grails makes this a snap to do.

"Configuration?" You may be wondering what happened to "convention over configuration." Well, keep in mind that it's *over*, not *instead of*, and, besides, no matter how hard Larry Ellison tries, there's still no convention for which database to use.[12] Also, Grails takes much of the pain out of the word *configuration* by allowing us to write all of our configuration code in Groovy instead of XML. The information about our database is in TekDays/grails-app/conf/DataSource.groovy. By default, it looks like this:

```
dataSource {
  pooled = true
  driverClassName = "org.hsqldb.jdbcDriver"
  username = "sa"
  password = ""
}
hibernate {
    cache.use_second_level_cache=true
    cache.use_query_cache=true
    cache.provider_class='com.opensymphony.oscache.hibernate.OSCacheProvider'
}
// environment specific settings
environments {
  development {
        dataSource {
                dbCreate = "create-drop" //one of 'create', 'create-drop','update'
                url = "jdbc:hsqldb:mem:devDB"
        }
  }
  test {
        dataSource {
                dbCreate = "update"
                url = "jdbc:hsqldb:mem:testDb"
        }
  }
  production {
        dataSource {
                dbCreate = "update"
                url = "jdbc:hsqldb:file:prodDb;shutdown=true"
        }
  }
}
```

---

12. Larry Ellison is the cofounder and CEO of Oracle, maker of the leading enterprise database. See http://en.wikipedia.org/wiki/Larry_Ellison.

Along with your basic database information and a bit of Hibernate-specific options, this file has three environment blocks. These can be used to configure our application to use different databases for development, test, and production. Changing from the default HsqlDb to MySQL requires changing only five lines and adding a .jar file to our project. For now, we'll focus on the development environment. Open TekDays/grails-app/conf/DataSource.groovy, and change it as indicated here:

```
beyond/TekDays/grails-app/conf/DataSource.groovy
dataSource {
        pooled = true
▶       driverClassName = "com.mysql.jdbc.Driver"
▶       username = "dave"
▶       password = "1234"
}
hibernate {
    cache.use_second_level_cache=true
    cache.use_query_cache=true
    cache.provider_class='com.opensymphony.oscache.hibernate.OSCacheProvider'
}
// environment specific settings
environments {
        development {
                dataSource {
▶                 dbCreate = "update"//one of 'create', 'create-drop','update'
▶                 url = "jdbc:mysql://localhost:3306/tekdays"
                }
        }
        test {
                dataSource {
                        dbCreate = "update"
                        url = "jdbc:hsqldb:mem:testDb"
                }
        }
        production {
                dataSource {
                        dbCreate = "update"
                        url = "jdbc:hsqldb:file:prodDb;shutdown=true"
                }
        }
}
```

Now we need to copy mysql-connector-java-5.0.7-bin.jar, which we can get from http://dev.mysql.com/downloads/connector/j/5.0.html, to the TekDays/lib directory. We also need to create an empty database called tekdays. Grails will create all the tables for us when we run the application for the first time.

One last note regarding the database: the first time we run the application with a real database, the bootstrap code will execute and create some initial data for us. Unless we remove it or code around it, this will happen *every time* we run the application. So, before we end up with a ton of duplicate data, it's a good idea to remove the bootstrap code after it has been run once or add code to ensure it will run only once. For example, we could wrap the code in Bootstrap.init() with an **if** block, like this:

```
if (!TekEvent.get(1)){
  //bootstrap code goes here...
}
```

With this code in place, the entire init block will be ignored after the first time it is run. To help with making changes once an application is in production, there are plug-ins available that enable database migrations.[13]

Before we leave this topic, I'll mention another strategy. Some choose to leave the development database as an HsqlDB in-memory database and provide persistent databases for test and production. In this case, we would make the bootstrap code conditional on environment instead of data. Here's an example of how to do this:

```
import grails.util.GrailsUtil
...
if (GrailsUtil.environment == 'development'){
  //bootstrap code goes here...
}
```

5.5 Summary

Our application is actually in roughly the same state as it was at the beginning of this chapter, but now we've armed ourselves with the knowledge and the code necessary to begin making major progress. In the next chapter, we will deal with some of the UI issues that were bothering our customer, and then we'll tackle the next feature on our list.

---

13. Autobase is one example of a Grails migration plug-in. Check it out at http://www.grails.org/plugin/autobase.

Chapter 6

Getting Things Done

In this iteration, we're going to take advantage of the generated scaffolding code to make our views more pleasing to our customer. We'll also work on implementing the task list features of TekDays so that TekDays users can get things done. Along the way, we'll learn just how easy it is to modify and extend Grails views.

6.1 Changing All Our Views at Once

We saw in the previous chapter how Grails uses SiteMesh to provide a consistent look throughout an application. That's what's been giving us that cool Grails logo on all of our views. But that's not quite what our customer wants for TekDays. Let's see what we can do about that. Open TekDays/grails-app/views/layout/main.gsp, and modify the following line:

```
<div class="logo">
  <img src="${resource(dir:'images',file:'td_logo.png')}" alt="TekDays"/>
</div>
```

Of course, you can substitute your own logo design, or you can download td_logo.png from the book's website. Talk about low-hanging fruit! Our new logo will now show up on every page of our application. In Figure 6.1, on the following page, we get a peek at what our pages will look like.

That's not all we can do in this file, but it's all we need to do for now. We could go on and add sidebars, a footer, a standard menu, and so on. But we don't want to get ahead of ourselves.

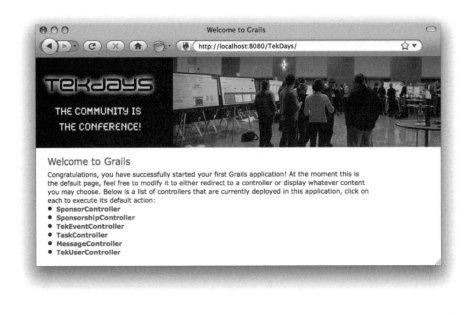

Figure 6.1: TEKDAYS HOME PAGE WITH NEW LOGO

Let's look at another file that is shared across all the views in our application. Grails puts the CSS code for all of the scaffolded views in web-app/css/main.css. We can change many aspects of our views by modifying this file. In an effort to keep style code out of our pages, we will be adding to this file for the small amount of additional CSS that we will be using in TekDays. The additional style rules that we are using can be found in Appendix A, on page 201. Now let's turn our attention to our scaffolded views.

6.2 Modifying the Scaffolded Views

We're going to go through the four scaffolded views of the TekEvent class and make some simple modifications. (The things we change here can just as easily be done for the other classes' views.) As we go through these changes, we can leave the application running and immediately see the changes by simply refreshing the browser—another example of how Grails keeps that rapid feedback loop going. This also takes the pain out of the tweaking process that we so often have to go through to get a page "just right."

The List View

One of the problems our customer pointed out earlier about the list view was that the id field is not something that the users need to see. It's easy enough to remove it, but it happens to also serve as our anchor for linking to the show view. We'll see how easy it is to move the anchor to a more sensible property. While we're at it, why don't we also remove the organizer from the table? It's not really something users will be concerned with as they look through a list of events.

Let's see what these changes look like. Open TekDays/grails-app/views/tekEvent/list.gsp, and go to the <*thead*> block. Remove the Id and Organizer columns. You should be left with this:

things/TekDays/grails-app/views/tekEvent/list.gsp

```
<thead>
  <tr>
    <g:sortableColumn property="name" title="Name" />
    <g:sortableColumn property="city" title="City" />
    <g:sortableColumn property="description" title="Description" />
    <g:sortableColumn property="venue" title="Venue" />
  </tr>
</thead>
```

This next step is almost as easy. In the <*tr*> block inside the <*g:each*> tag, modify the code as shown here:

things/TekDays/grails-app/views/tekEvent/list.gsp

```
<tr class="${(i % 2) == 0 ? 'odd' : 'even'}">
  <td>
▶     <g:link action="show" id="${tekEventInstance.id}">
▶       ${fieldValue(bean:tekEventInstance, field:'name')}
▶     </g:link></td>
    <td>${fieldValue(bean:tekEventInstance, field:'city')}</td>
    <td>${fieldValue(bean:tekEventInstance, field:'description')}</td>
    <td>${fieldValue(bean:tekEventInstance, field:'venue')}</td>
  </tr>
```

We removed the organizer column first. Then, in order to preserve the <*g:link*> tag around the id, we actually removed the name column and changed the field attribute in the first column from id to name. Now when we refresh the page, it will look like Figure 6.2, on the following page.

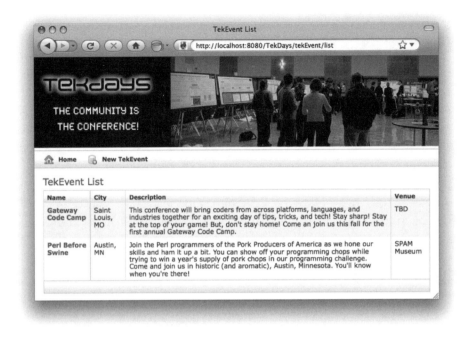

Figure 6.2: MODIFIED TEKEVENT LIST VIEW

The Show View

The show view presents several opportunities for improvement. We'll go through from top to bottom and fix things up. You can save the file and refresh after each step, and we'll show the new view when we're done. Open TekDays/grails-app/views/tekEvent/show.gsp, and let's get started.

Near the top of this file you'll see an *<h1>* tag containing the text "Show TekEvent." Let's replace that text with the name of the event:

things/TekDays/grails-app/views/tekEvent/show.gsp

```
<h1>${fieldValue(bean:tekEventInstance, field: 'name')}</h1>
```

This is an example of how we can use Groovy expressions anywhere on a page.

Next, let's remove the id property from the main part of the page. Notice that each property is displayed within a *<tr>* tag; just remove the opening *<tr>*, the closing *</tr>*, and everything in between. Repeat this process for any other properties you want to remove—for example, the name property, since we already have it displayed in the heading.

We'll leave description alone. We'll move the organizer down directly before the volunteers. Then we'll do something a little more clever for the city property:

things/TekDays/grails-app/views/tekEvent/show.gsp

```
<tr class="prop">
▶   <td valign="top" class="name">Location:</td>
    <td valign="top" class="value">
▶     ${fieldValue(bean:tekEventInstance, field:'venue')},
▶     ${fieldValue(bean:tekEventInstance, field:'city')}
    </td>
</tr>
```

We changed the label, which is the value in the first *<td>*, to "Location," and we included the venue in the same line.

Next we'll tackle the date properties. The way they're currently being displayed is not going to cut it. I mean, sure people will want their events to run on schedule, but I doubt they're going to worry about the exact hour, minute, and second that it starts.

things/TekDays/grails-app/views/tekEvent/show.gsp

```
<tr class="prop">
    <td valign="top" class="name">Start Date:</td>
    <td valign="top" class="value">
▶     <g:formatDate format="MMMM dd, yyyy"
▶                   date="${tekEventInstance.startDate}"/>
    </td>
</tr>
```

Here we replaced the fieldValue method call on the startDate property with the *<formatDate>* GSP tag.[1] Do the same with the endDate property.

things/TekDays/grails-app/views/tekEvent/show.gsp

```
<tr class="prop">
    <td valign="top" class="name">End Date:</td>
    <td valign="top" class="value">
▶     <g:formatDate format="MMMM dd, yyyy"
▶                   date="${tekEventInstance.endDate}"/>
    </td>
</tr>
```

Finally, let's clean up the way the Sponsorship collection is displayed. Recall from the discussion in Section 4.6, *Many-to-Many Relationships*, on page 58, that we did not declare a toString() method because the

---

1. See http://grails.org/doc/1.1.x/ref/Tags/formatDate.html.

way we display a Sponsorship will depend on the context. That's why it currently shows up as "Sponsorship:1." Since we're working on the TekEvent views, we'll modify the display with that context in mind.

```
things/TekDays/grails-app/views/tekEvent/show.gsp
<tr class="prop">
  <td valign="top" class="name">Sponsored By:</td>
  <td valign="top" style="text-align:left;" class="value">
    <ul>
      <g:each var="s" in="${tekEventInstance.sponsorships}">
        <li><g:link controller="sponsorship" action="show" id="${s.id}">
          ${s.sponsor?.encodeAsHTML()}
        </g:link></li>
      </g:each>
    </ul>
  </td>
</tr>
```

All we had to do was change the s.encodeAsHTML() to s.sponsor.encodeAs-HTML(). If this was the Sponsor show view, we would change it to s.event.encodeAsHTML(). Take a look at Figure 6.3, on the facing page, to see the results of our changes.

The Create View

The create view doesn't need too much work. One thing we can do is fix the way date properties are handled. Open TekDays/grails-app/views/tekEvent/create.gsp, and zero in on the <g:datePicker> tag used for the startDate property.

```
things/TekDays/grails-app/views/tekEvent/create.gsp
<tr class="prop">
  <td valign="top" class="name">
    <label for="startDate">Start Date:</label>
  </td>
  <td valign="top" class="value $
    {hasErrors(bean:tekEventInstance,field:'startDate','errors')}">
    <g:datePicker name="startDate" precision="day"
                  value="${tekEventInstance?.startDate}" >
    </g:datePicker>
  </td>
</tr>
```

The <g:datePicker> tag can take a precision attribute, which will allow us to fine-tune the display. The valid values are year, month, day, hour, and minute. We set ours to day, and you can see the effects in Figure 6.4, on page 98.

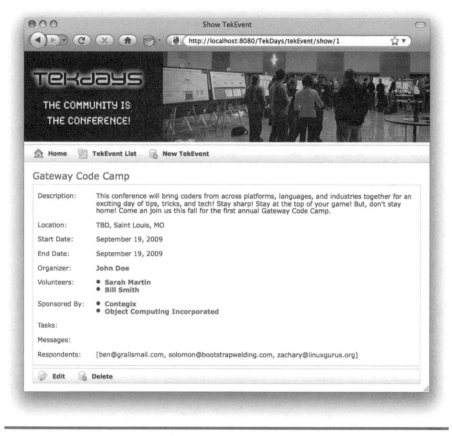

Figure 6.3: MODIFIED TEKEVENT SHOW VIEW

The Edit View

The edit view needs only the sponsorship change that we made in the show view and the precision attribute for the *<g:datePicker>* tag, as we did for the create view. See the following code:

```
things/TekDays/grails-app/views/tekEvent/edit.gsp
              <tr class="prop">
                <td valign="top" class="name">
                  <label for="startDate">Start Date:</label>
                </td>
                <td valign="top" class="value
                    ${hasErrors(bean:tekEventInstance,field:'startDate','errors')}">
                  <g:datePicker name="startDate" precision="day"
                      value="${tekEventInstance?.startDate}" >
                  </g:datePicker>
                </td>
              </tr>
```

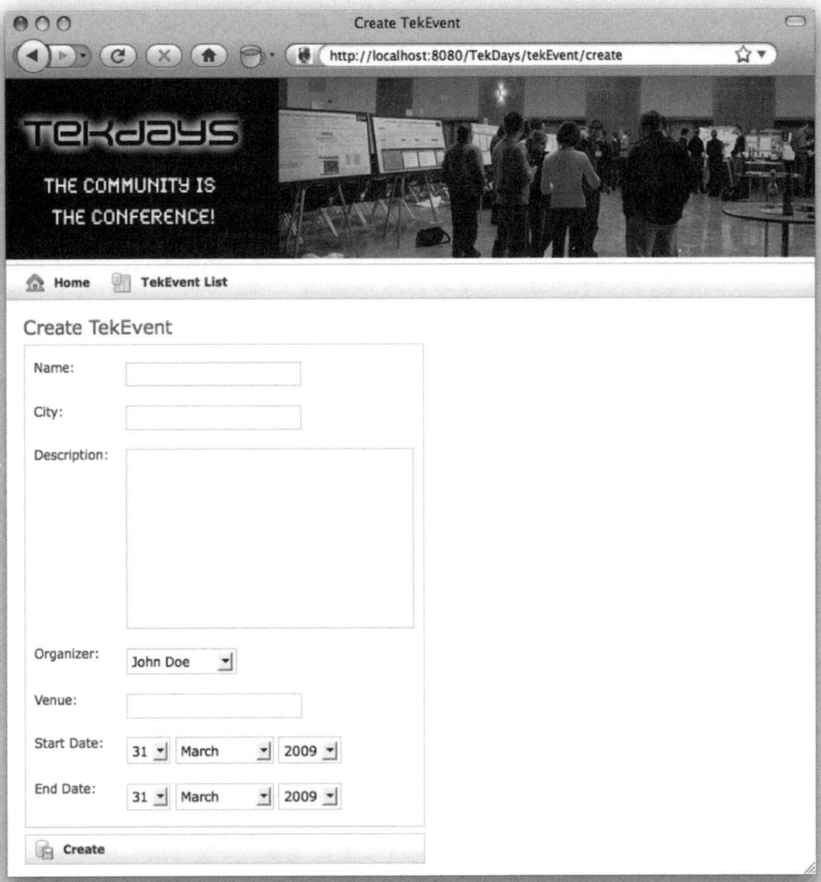

Figure 6.4: MODIFIED TEKEVENT CREATE VIEW

```
                        <tr class="prop">
                          <td valign="top" class="name">
                            <label for="endDate">End Date:</label>
                          </td>
                          <td valign="top" class="value
                              ${hasErrors(bean:tekEventInstance,field:'endDate','errors')}">
                            <g:datePicker name="endDate" precision="day"
                                          value="${tekEventInstance?.endDate}">
                            </g:datePicker>
                          </td>
                        </tr>
```

▶

things/TekDays/grails-app/views/tekEvent/edit.gsp

```
<tr class="prop">
  <td valign="top" class="name">
    <label for="sponsorships">Sponsorships:</label>
  </td>
  <td valign="top" class="value
      ${hasErrors(bean:tekEventInstance,field:'sponsorships','errors')}">
    <ul>
      <g:each var="s" in="${tekEventInstance?.sponsorships?}">
        <li>
          <g:link controller="sponsorship" action="show"
                  id="${s.id}">${s.sponsor?.encodeAsHTML()}</g:link>
        </li>
      </g:each>
    </ul>
    <g:link controller="sponsorship"
            params="['tekEvent.id':tekEventInstance?.id]"
            action="create">
      Add Sponsorship
    </g:link>
  </td>
</tr>
```

The new and improved edit view looks like Figure 6.5, on the following page.

We may return to some of these views later, but for now things are looking much nicer. Now that *we've* gotten some things done, we'll move on to the next feature in our list. We'll add a task list to our application so that our *users* can get things done.

6.3 Event Task List

According to our feature list, we need to be able to add and remove tasks, assign tasks, and have a default set of tasks. We already have the add and remove bit done: we have the same four scaffolded views

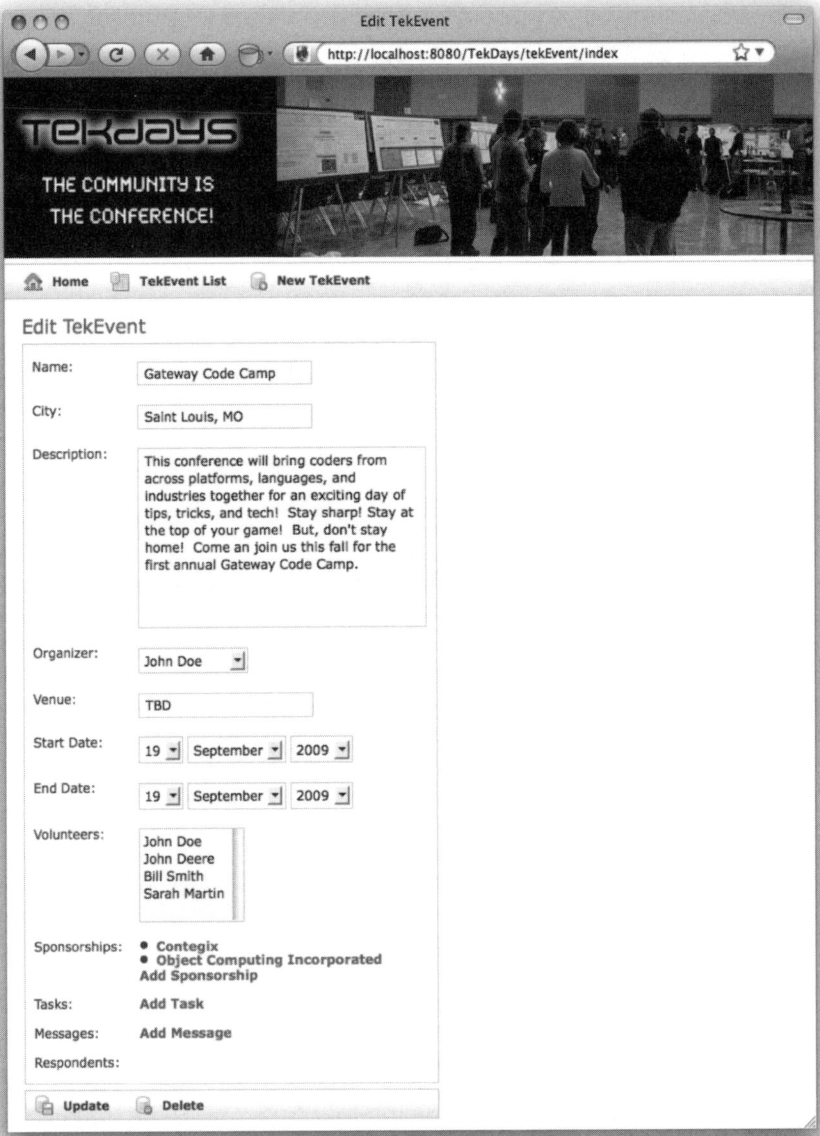

Figure 6.5: MODIFIED TekEvent EDIT VIEW

for the Task that we have for the TekEvent. They were created when we ran the generate-all script.

As we see in Figure 6.5, on the preceding page, the TekEvent edit view provides a link labeled "Add Task," which brings up the Task create view. The Task edit view already contains a Delete link to remove tasks. So, we'll focus on providing a default set of tasks for a new event.

The task list feature will enable users to keep track of the many things that need to be done to put on a successful technical conference. Tasks will be assigned to volunteers, but the list will be available to the whole team. It's important to keep an eye on those details, or they'll fall through the cracks. According to our customer, most of the users will not have experience organizing an event of this magnitude. The idea behind the default tasks, then, is to give them some ideas and a starting point.

Our customer has provided us with a set of default tasks. Rather than listing them here, we'll practice the DRY principle.[2] We'll list the default tasks in the code that we write to create them. Now we need to figure out where to put that code.

6.4 Grails Service Classes

We're going to write a method that will create several Task instances and add them to the tasks property of a newly created TekEvent. We will define this method in a *service* class. A Grails service class is a Plain Old Groovy Object (POGO) located in the grails-app/services directory and with a name ending in *Service*. By following these conventions, this plain old Groovy object will be endowed with magical powers.

Service classes are a great way to keep extra code out of our controllers. When we have application logic that doesn't fit well in any a domain class—for example, logic that involves multiple domain classes—it is tempting to add this code to the controller. Doing this can lead to bloated controllers that are difficult to read and maintain. To keep our controller leaner, we can move this type of application logic into service methods. We can't give a full treatment of service classes here, but we'll

---

2. DRY stands for Don't Repeat Yourself. This is one of the core principles in *The Pragmatic Programmer* [HT00].

discuss some of their features as we put them to use.[3] Of course, Grails provides a convenience script to create a new service class. Let's try it:

```
$ grails create-service Task
```

We called our service TaskService because we're going to use it to create Task instances. Before we get started with that, let's take a look at what Grails created for us:

things/TekDays/grails-app/services/TaskService.groovy

```
class TaskService {

    boolean transactional = true

    def serviceMethod() {

    }
}
```

We start with a stubbed-out method called serviceMethod() and a boolean transactional property, which is defaulted to true. This property will cause any method declared in this class to be executed within a transaction.[4] That's all we have to do to enable transactions; the rest is handled behind the scenes by Spring and Hibernate. If you've ever had to code transaction handling in a web application, I'll give you a moment to get your jaw off the floor.

Now let's add a method to TaskService called addDefaultTasks(tekEvent). Open TekDays/grails-app/services/TaskService.groovy, and add the following code:

things/TekDays/grails-app/services/TaskService.groovy

```
def addDefaultTasks(tekEvent){
  if (tekEvent.tasks?.size() > 0)
    return //We only want to add tasks to a new event

  tekEvent.addToTasks new Task(title:'Identify potential venues')
  tekEvent.addToTasks new Task(title:'Get price / availability of venues')
  tekEvent.addToTasks new Task(title:'Compile potential sponsor list')
  tekEvent.addToTasks new Task(title:'Design promotional materials')
  tekEvent.addToTasks new Task(title:'Compile potential advertising avenues')
  tekEvent.addToTasks new Task(title:'Locate swag provider (preferably local)')
  tekEvent.save()
}
```

---

3. You can find more details on Grails service classes at http://tinyurl.com/grails-service-layer.
4. See http://en.wikipedia.org/wiki/Transaction_(database).

Let's walk through this code. First, we check to see whether the tekEvent passed in has anything in its tasks collection. If it does, then we bail. Otherwise, we begin a series of calls to tekEvent.addToTasks(). This method is one of the many added dynamically by Grails. (Notice that we're taking advantage of the optional parentheses to reduce the noise in our code.) Finally, we call tekEvent.save(), which will cascade to save all the Task instances too.

That's it for our service class, but now we need to use it. The logical place to do that would be in the save action of the TekEventController; that way, we can be sure that the default tasks will be added to every TekEvent that is successfully saved. Open TekDays/grails-app/controllers/ TekEventController.groovy, and add this single property declaration at the top of the class:

things/TekDays/grails-app/controllers/TekEventController.groovy

```
class TekEventController {

    def taskService
    def index = { redirect(action:list,params:params) }
```

All we have to do is to declare a property named after the service class (with the first letter lowercase), and an instance of that class will be injected into our controller at runtime. That's *autowiring* Grails style, and it's pretty awesome! We don't need to create an instance of TaskService and assign it to our controller, and we don't need to worry about ensuring that it exists before we call it. It's all managed for us by Grails, courtesy of "convention over configuration."

Now in the save action, we'll add the call to addDefaultTasks():

things/TekDays/grails-app/controllers/TekEventController.groovy

```
def save = {
    def tekEventInstance = new TekEvent(params)
    if(!tekEventInstance.hasErrors() && tekEventInstance.save()) {
        flash.message = "TekEvent ${tekEventInstance.id} created"
        taskService.addDefaultTasks(tekEventInstance)
        redirect(action:show,id:tekEventInstance.id)
    }
    else {
        render(view: 'create',model:[tekEventInstance:tekEventInstance])
    }
}
```

We put the call after the validation and saving of the TekEvent, so we don't waste effort trying to add tasks to a TekEvent that won't save. If it does save successfully, we'll see the default tasks loaded.

Figure 6.6: TEKEVENT SHOW VIEW WITH DEFAULT TASKS

If we create a new event now, we should see something like Figure 6.6.

Before we move on from here, let's write a test for our new service class. Grails has already created a stubbed-out test class for us in Tek-Days/test/unit/TaskServiceTests.groovy. We will use that file, but first we'll move it to the integration test directory: TekDays/test/integration.

6.5 Integration Testing

By putting a test class in the integration test directory, we turn it into an *integration test*. An integration test is a JUnit test case, just like a

Grails unit test. The difference is in what is available to the test at run-time. Unit tests are meant to test a unit (class) in isolation, so Grails doesn't give unit tests any of its dynamic goodness. Integration tests are meant to test multiple classes working together. When running integration tests, Grails adds all of the dynamic behavior that we're taking advantage of in our application.

Since the process of adding default tasks to an event involves the TaskService, Task, and TekEvent classes, an integration test is a good fit. Let's write our test. Open TekDays/test/integration/TaskServiceTests.groovy, and add the following code:

things/TekDays/test/integration/TaskServiceTests.groovy

```
import grails.test.*

class TaskServiceTests extends GrailsUnitTestCase {
    def taskService

    protected void setUp() {
        super.setUp()
        new TekUser(fullName:'Tammy Tester',
                    userName:'tester',
                    email:'tester@test.com',
                    website:'test.com',
                    bio:'A test person').save()
    }

    protected void tearDown() {
        super.tearDown()
    }

    void testAddDefaultTasks() {
        def e = new TekEvent(name:'Test Event',
                             city:'TestCity, USA',
                             description:'Test Description',
                             organizer:TekUser.findByUserName('tester'),
                             venue:'TestCenter',
                             startDate:new Date(),
                             endDate:new Date() + 1)
        taskService.addDefaultTasks(e)
        assertEquals e.tasks.size(), 6
    }
}
```

At the top of this file, we declare a taskService property, just like we did in the TekEventController. Then in the setUp() method, we create and save a TekUser. We have to do this because the organizer property of TekEvent does not accept nulls; we need a real TekUser to assign to that prop-

Test Data Source

Integration tests will use the data source for the *test* environment. Before running integration tests, you may want to set the data source for the *test* environment to a persistent database. For an example, refer to Section 5.4, *Configuring a Database*, on page 86.

erty. Then, in the testAddDefaultTasks() method (the test), we're creating a TekEvent and passing it to the taskService.addDefaultTasks() method. Finally, we assert() that our event's tasks property contains the same number of items as our service method is adding.

We can run all of our tests now with grails test-app, and we should see all our tests pass. That's a good feeling!

6.6 Modifying the Task Class

Great! We now have default tasks on all new events, users can add and remove tasks as needed, and tasks can be assigned to users. But there's something missing....

Excuse me while I take off my customer hat and smack myself in the forehead.

We don't have any way to mark a task as completed! Not to worry—we'll just do a quick bit of reworking, and we'll be good to go. First we'll modify the Task class. Open TekDays/grails-app/domain/Task.groovy, and add a new property and constraint, as shown here:

things/TekDays/grails-app/domain/Task.groovy

```
class Task {
    String title
    String notes
    TekUser assignedTo
    Date dueDate
    TekEvent event
▶   Boolean completed

    static constraints = {
        title(blank:false)
        notes(blank:true, nullable:true, maxSize:5000)
        assignedTo(nullable:true)
```

```
        dueDate(nullable:true)
►       completed(nullable:true)
    }

    static belongsTo = TekEvent

    String toString(){
        title
    }
}
```

Now that we have a completed property to work with, let's modify our views to take advantage of it. Open TekDays/grails-app/views/task/show.gsp, and add a *<tr>* block at the bottom of the *<tbody>*, like so:

things/TekDays/grails-app/views/task/show.gsp

```
    <tr class="prop">
      <td valign="top" class="name">Completed:</td>
      <td valign="top" class="value">
        ${fieldValue(bean:taskInstance, field:'completed')}
      </td>
    </tr>
</tbody>
```

That will allow our users to see when a Task is completed.

Next, open TekDays/grails-app/views/task/edit.gsp, and add the following *<tr>* block at the bottom of the *<tbody>*, as we just did with the show view:

things/TekDays/grails-app/views/task/edit.gsp

```
    <tr class="prop">
      <td valign="top" class="name">
       <label for="completed">Completed:</label>
      </td>
      <td valign="top">
        <g:checkBox name="completed" value="${taskInstance?.completed}"/>
      </td>
    </tr>
</tbody>
```

This will add a checkbox to our edit view so that users can mark a task as completed (see Figure 6.7, on the following page).

6.7 Summary

Well, this was a productive iteration. We implemented our task-related features. Along the way, we learned about Grails service classes, integration testing, and what it takes to modify or extend a Grails domain

Figure 6.7: TASK EDIT VIEW

class after we've generated the code. Take a break. You deserve it! Catch up on some blogs (http://groovyblogs.org would be a good choice) or email. Next we will work on adding a message forum and see what we can learn while we're at it.

Chapter 7

Forum Messages and UI Tricks

A technical event, like any collaborative project, will turn out better if the communication flows freely. To help facilitate this for our users, we're going to include a forum where the organizer and volunteers can post and reply to messages. Then, to make it easy for new volunteers to come up to speed on what's going on, we'll include a threaded view of all past messages. That's the goal of this iteration. While we're at it, we'll learn more about the interaction between controllers and views, we'll get an introduction to GSP templates, and we'll get a look at Ajax, Grails style.

We won't have to start from scratch, because Grails has already given us the list, create, show, and edit views to work with. The create view (see Figure 7.1, on the next page), for example, gives us everything we need to create a new message.

We need to change a few things to turn these scaffolded pages into a usable message forum. Our users should be able to see messages in a more logical manner than a plain list. They'll also need the ability to reply to a message they are reading, preferably without leaving the page.

7.1 Restricting Messages to an Event

Since we want the messages to constitute a forum for a given event, we will have to modify the scaffolded views to limit the viewing and creating of Message instances to the TekEvent that they relate to. It's important to note that the relationship between TekEvent and Message is already

Figure 7.1: SCAFFOLDED CREATE VIEW

established in the domain model; we're just going to make the workflow match that relationship.

We'll start by modifying the event show view. Where we currently have an unordered list of Message instances displayed in this view, we are going to have a single hyperlink that will lead to the message list view. Further, we are going to filter the list to show only those Message instances that are related to that TekEvent.

Open TekDays/grails-app/views/tekEvent/show.gsp, and replace the code in
the Messages<*tr*> tag with the following <*g:link*> tag:

forum/TekDays/grails-app/views/tekEvent/show.gsp

```
<tr class="prop">
  <td valign="top" class="name">Messages:</td>
  <td  valign="top" style="text-align:left;" class="value">
    <g:link controller="message" action="list" id="${tekEventInstance.id}">
      View Messages
    </g:link>
  </td>
</tr>
```

The <*g:link*> tag will create a link to the list action of the MessageController and will pass a TekEvent.id. If you follow this link now, it will bring
you to the message list, but the TekEvent.id will be ignored.

To fix that, we'll modify the list action in the MessageController. Open
TekDays/grails-app/controllers/MessageController.groovy, and modify the list
action as follows:

forum/TekDays/grails-app/controllers/MessageController.groovy

```
def list = {
    params.max = Math.min( params.max ? params.max.toInteger() : 10,  100)
    def list
    def count
    def event = TekEvent.get(params.id)
    if (event){
        list = Message.findAllByEvent(event, params)
        count = Message.countByEvent(event)
    }
    else{
        list = Message.list(params)
        count = Message.count()
    }
    [messageInstanceList: list, messageInstanceTotal: count, event: event]
}
```

We first declare list and count variables to be used in the Map at the end
of the action. Then we declare an event variable and attempt to assign
a TekEvent to it, using the id that was passed in from the link in the
event show view. If a TekEvent is found, then we load the list and count
variables using dynamic methods provided by GORM. If event is null, we
fall back to the original means of retrieving the list and count. Finally, we
assign list and count to their appropriate keys in the return Map, and we
add the event:event key/value pair to the Map. This last step will make
the TekEvent instance available to us in the list view.

Now we'll turn our attention to the message list view. If we navigate to this view using the link we just modified on the event show view, we'll only see messages related to a single event. That's great, but if we click the New Message button, we'll need to explicitly choose the event on the message create view. We want that to be loaded automatically, and we can do it by modifying a single line of code. Let's open TekDays/grails-app/views/message/list.gsp and modify the New Message <g:link> tag, like so:

forum/TekDays/grails-app/views/message/list.gsp

```
<g:link class="create" action="create"
    params='["event.id":"${event?.id}"]'>New Message
</g:link>
```

All we did here was add a params attribute to the <g:link> tag. This attribute is a Map containing parameters to be added to the URL created by the <g:link> tag. We then assign event.id to a key of the same name. (Since the key contains a "." we had to put it in quotes.) This will result in a parameter like event.id=2. Grails' binding will use that to retrieve a TekEvent instance and assign it to the Message.event property. All of that and more is done with the following single line. Slick stuff!

```
messageInstance.properties = params
```

Open TekDays/grails-app/views/message/create.gsp, and follow along as we make a few changes, starting with the Message List button. We'll do the same thing to that one that we did to the one on the TekEvent show view.

forum/TekDays/grails-app/views/message/create.gsp

```
<span class="menuButton">
  <g:link class="list" action="list" id="${messageInstance?.event?.id}">
    Message List
  </g:link>
</span>
```

That will ensure that we stay with this event's messages if we return to the list from here.

Now we'll add the name of the event to the page heading. Modify the <h1> tag to look like this:

forum/TekDays/grails-app/views/message/create.gsp

```
<h1>${messageInstance?.event?.name} Forum - New Message</h1>
```

Since we have the event name there and since we don't want to change the event from the page, let's replace the <tr> tag containing the event property with a hidden *<input>*. We don't need to display the event again, but we do need to have the value in the *<form>* so that it will be submitted when we save.

forum/TekDays/grails-app/views/message/create.gsp

```
<input type="hidden" name="event.id" value="${messageInstance?.event?.id}" />
```

Choosing what message you're replying to while creating the message doesn't make much sense, so let's remove that *<tr>* tag too. In its place, we'll add a label inside a conditional block; that way, if this is a reply, we'll say so. Let's put this at the top of the page for clarity. Add the following code immediately after the opening *<tbody>* tag:

forum/TekDays/grails-app/views/message/create.gsp

```
<g:if test="${messageInstance.parent}">
  <tr class="prop">
      <td valign="top" class="name">
          <label>In Reply to:</label>
      </td>
      <td valign="top" class="value">
          ${messageInstance.parent.author}
      </td>
  </tr>
</g:if>
```

Here we used a *<g:if>* tag to prevent this from being rendered unless the messageInstance has a parent property. The rest of this code just renders a label and the author of the parent Message. (We won't see this feature yet since we don't yet have a way to create replies, but we'll get there soon enough.)

Finally, we'll use a little CSS to give our users more room to write their messages. Add class="messageField" to the subject *<input>* and the content*<textarea>*, like so:

forum/TekDays/grails-app/views/message/create.gsp

```
<tr class="prop">
    <td valign="top" class="name">
        <label for="subject">Subject:</label>
    </td>
    <td valign="top"
        class="value ${hasErrors(bean:messageInstance,field:'subject','errors')}">
        <input type="text" class="messageField" id="subject" name="subject"
            value="${fieldValue(bean:messageInstance,field:'subject')}"/>
    </td>
</tr>
```

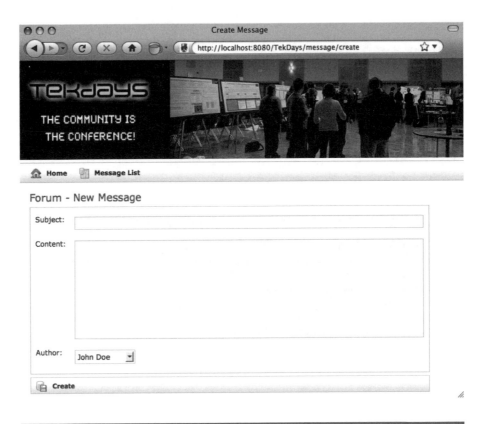

Figure 7.2: CREATE VIEW 2.0 (SO TO SPEAK)

```
<tr class="prop">
    <td valign="top" class="name">
        <label for="content">Content:</label>
    </td>
    <td valign="top"
        class="value ${hasErrors(bean:messageInstance,field:'content','errors')}">
      <textarea class="messageField" rows="5" cols="60" name="content">
        ${fieldValue(bean:messageInstance, field:'content')}
      </textarea>
    </td>
</tr>
```

In Figure 7.2, we see our new create view. That's much better. Next up: cleaning up the list and show views.

7.2 Of Templates and Ajax

On second thought, instead of cleaning up the list and show views, let's just set them aside and create a new view that will replace them both. To do that, we'll take advantage of Grails' GSP templates.

GSP templates are simply chunks of GSP code in a file that begins with an underscore (_likethis.gsp). They provide an easy way to share common code across multiple pages. You can include a GSP template in a GSP page with the *<g:render>* tag, like this:

```
<g:render template="someTemplate" />
```

This line would render a template called _someTemplate.gsp in the same directory as the page that it is being called from. To render templates from a different directory, add the path before the name of the template. We never include the "_" at the beginning of the template name in the *<g:render>* tag.

Another popular use for GSP templates is rendering the response to Ajax calls; that's what we're after here. Before we get too much further, let me lay out the plan. What we want is a single page with a list of messages in the upper section, and fields for viewing a single message in the lower section. When a user selects a message in the list, that message's values will display in the fields below, without reloading the rest of the page. Pretty cool, huh? Our customer sure thought so (if I do say so myself). Now let's see how easy this can be with Grails.

To get started, let's create TekDays/grails-app/views/message/ajaxList.gsp. As a shortcut, just copy TekDays/grails-app/views/message/list.gsp, and remove most of it. Keep the *<html>* and *<head>* (with contents), and in the *<body>*, keep the first *<div>*. You should end up with something that looks like this:

forum/TekDays/grails-app/views/message/ajaxList.gsp

```
<html>

  <head>
    <meta http-equiv="Content-Type" content="text/html; charset=UTF-8"/>
    <meta name="layout" content="main" />
    <title>Messages</title>
  </head>
  <body>
    <div class="nav">
      <span class="menuButton">
        <a class="home" href="${resource(dir:'')}">Home</a>
      </span>
```

```
    <span class="menuButton">
      <g:link class="create" action="create"
          params='[eventId:"${event?.id}"]'>New Message
      </g:link>
    </span>
  </div>

</body>
</html>
```

We kept the <head> section from the list because it contains a couple of
<meta> tags that we need. Since this new view is going to replace the
list view, it makes sense to keep the same button bar. Other than that,
we kept only the basic page structure tags.

To flesh out the body of our new view, add the following code right after
that </div> tag:

`forum/TekDays/grails-app/views/message/ajaxList.gsp`

```
<div class="body">
  <h1>${event?.name} - Forum Messages</h1>
  <div id="messageList">
    <g:each in="${messageInstanceList}" var="messageInstance">
    </g:each>
  </div>
  <h3>Message Details</h3>
  <div id="details">
  </div>
</div>
```

First we added a <div> with class="body" to be consistent with the other
pages in our application, and then we added an <h1> tag, similar to the
one on the create view, using the TekEvent instance that will be passed
in from the controller. Then we added a <div>, with an ID of messageList,
to hold the list of messages. We have a style rule in main.css for this ID
that will provide scrolling if our list gets that long. (See Appendix A, on
page 201.) Inside this <div>, we have a <g:each> tag, which will iterate
over the messageInstanceList. Whatever we put in the body of that tag will
be displayed once for each element in the list. We'll talk about what to
put there shortly.

Below the list <div>, we added an <h3> tag to serve as a heading to the
message detail portion of the page. Finally, we added a <div> with an
id of details. This is where the message detail template that we are about
to create will be rendered.

Creating the Template

Now we need to create the template that will display an individual message. This time, just create a blank file called _details.gsp in the TekDays/grails-app/views/message directory. We'll borrow the *<div>*, *<table>*, and three *<tr>* tags from TekDays/grails-app/views/message/ show.gsp. (The three *<tr>* tags are for the subject, content, and author properties.) Since this file's code will be inserted into another page, it doesn't need its own *<html>* or *<head>* tags.

forum/TekDays/grails-app/views/message/_details.gsp

```
<div class="dialog">
  <table>
    <tr class="prop">
      <td valign="top" class="name">Subject:</td>
      <td valign="top" class="value">
        ${fieldValue(bean:messageInstance, field:'subject')}
      </td>
    </tr>
    <tr class="prop">
      <td valign="top" class="name">Content:</td>
      <td valign="top" class="value">
        ${fieldValue(bean:messageInstance, field:'content')}
      </td>
    </tr>
    <tr class="prop">
      <td valign="top" class="name">Author:</td>
      <td valign="top" class="value">
        <g:link controller="tekUser" action="show"
            id="${messageInstance?.author?.id}">
          ${messageInstance?.author?.encodeAsHTML()}
        </g:link>
      </td>
    </tr>
  </table>
  <div class="buttons">
    <span class="menuButton">
      <g:link class="create" action="reply" id="${messageInstance?.id}">
        Reply
      </g:link>
    </span>
  </div>
</div>
```

You may have noticed that we also added a Reply "button" at the bottom of the template. This is actually a *<g:link>* that will be styled to look like a button. The *<g:link>* will call the reply action—which we still need to create. Don't let me forget to return to that.

Looking at the code for our template, we can see that the only data element that it will need is a Message instance called (believe it or not) messageInstance. This is important to note, because when a template is rendered, the data it requires needs to be passed to it. A template cannot automatically see the data elements of the page that renders it. We'll look at how to provide the data to the template in the next section as we see how to render our template in response to an Ajax call.

Ajax in Grails

Grails includes several Ajax tags, which we can use to call a controller action and update a page element with the results. That's exactly what we need to do, but before we do it, let's discuss a bit about the way that Grails Ajax tags work.

Grails supports a variety of popular JavaScript libraries with regard to its Ajax tags.[1] To use these tags, we need to tell Grails which library we are using. We do this with the *<g:javascript>* tag and its library attribute. This tag is placed in the *<head>* section of a page. Let's go back to TekDays/grails-app/views/message/ajaxList.gsp and add the following line to the *<head>*:

forum/TekDays/grails-app/views/message/ajaxList.gsp

```
<g:javascript library="prototype" />
```

Now we can use one of Grails' Ajax tags, and it will adapt to use the Prototype library.[2] The tag we're going to use is *<g:remoteLink>*.

Let's see how this looks in our code, and then we'll discuss what it's doing. In TekDays/grails-app/views/message/ajaxList.gsp, add the following code to the *<g:each>* body in our list*<div>*:

forum/TekDays/grails-app/views/message/ajaxList.gsp

```
        <g:each in="${messageInstanceList}" var="messageInstance">
►         <g:remoteLink action="showDetail" id="${messageInstance?.id}"
►             update="details">
►           ${messageInstance.author.fullName} - ${messageInstance.subject}
►         </g:remoteLink>
        </g:each>
```

---

1. See the Grails website for a list of supported libraries: http://www.grails.org/Ajax.
2. Grails handles any differences that might exist in the way different JavaScript libraries handle the tasks involved in the Ajax tags; the behavior of these tags is the same regardless of which of the supported libraries we use.

The <g:remoteLink> tag can take controller, action, and id attributes. If
the controller attribute is not provided, then the controller that rendered
the current page will be used by default. Since the ajaxList view will
be rendered by the MessageController, we don't need to specify it here.
We did give it an action attribute, which points to an action (which we
will create next in the MessageController). Then for the id, we use the
messageInstance variable from the <g:each>. The final attribute that we
set on the <g:remoteLink> tag is update. This attribute contains the ID
of the HTML element on this page that will be updated with the result
of the action—in this case, details.

For the body of the <g:remoteLink>, we used the messageInstance variable to build a string containing the name of the message's author and
the subject of the message. We'll see how this looks shortly, but first we
have to create the showDetail action. Open TekDays/grails-app/controllers/
MessageController.groovy, and add the following action:

forum/TekDays/grails-app/controllers/MessageController.groovy

```
def showDetail = {
    def messageInstance = Message.get(params.id)
    if (messageInstance) {
        render(template:"details", model:[messageInstance:messageInstance])
    }
    else {
        render "No message found with id: ${params.id}"
    }
}
```

This action expects the params to contain an id value. The first thing
we do is define a messageInstance variable and retrieve a Message using
the id value in the params. If we have a valid instance, we call the ren-
der() method and pass it the name of a template ("details") and a model,
which is a Map. The model parameter is used to provide the data that
the template will need. In this case, we have only one object in the
model, but we can include as many objects as our template needs. The
render() method will merge our template with the data in the message-
Instance bean and return the results as HTML. This HTML will then
replace the contents of the <div> on our page.

Now there's just one thing left to do before we can marvel at our handiwork: we need to provide a way to reach our new view. If we added
an action to the MessageController called ajaxList, it would automatically
render our new view, but it would just be a copy of the list action, and
that wouldn't be very DRY. So, we'll use a different approach. The same

render() method that we just used for our details template can be used
to render an entire view. Let's return to the list action in TekDays/grails-
app/controllers/MessageController.groovy and modify the last line (the line
that returns the Map):

```
forum.1/TekDays/grails-app/controllers/MessageController.groovy

def list = {
    params.max = Math.min( params.max ? params.max.toInteger() : 10,   100)
    def list
    def count
    def event = TekEvent.get(params.id)
    if (event){
        list = Message.findAllByEvent(event, params)
        count = Message.countByEvent(event)
    }
    else{
        list = Message.list(params)
        count = Message.count()
    }
    render(view:'ajaxList',
            model:[messageInstanceList: list, messageInstanceTotal: count,
                    event: event])
}
```

This time, we pass a view parameter instead of a template. We set that
parameter to our new page, and then we pass the existing Map as the
model. Now when the list action is called (for example, when we navigate to http://localhost:8080/TekDays/message/list), our new view will be
rendered.

Wait a minute. We still need to add a reply action to the MessageController. OK. The reply action will be very similar to the create action,
except that it will set the parent of the *new* Message to the *current* one. I
hope you still have MessageController.groovy open so you can slip in the
following code:

```
forum.1/TekDays/grails-app/controllers/MessageController.groovy

def reply = {
    def parent = Message.get(params.id)
    def messageInstance = new Message(parent:parent, event:parent.event,
                                        subject:"RE: $parent.subject")
    render(view:'create', model:['messageInstance':messageInstance])
}
```

In this action, we take the id parameter that is passed in on the link
from the ajaxList view and use it to retrieve a Message instance. Then
we create a new Message, setting its parent and subject properties based
on the retrieved instance. Finally, we use the render() method to render

the create view with the messageInstance in the model. This will open the create view, which we will now modify to handle this new responsibility.

When the create view is rendered from the reply action, the message will have a parent assigned. We'll change our view slightly and check for the existence of this property. Open the TekDays/grails-app/views/message/ create.gsp file, and add the following code right after the <*tbody*> tag:

```
forum.1/TekDays/grails-app/views/message/create.gsp
<g:if test="${messageInstance.parent}">
  <input type="hidden" name="parent.id" value="${messageInstance.parent.id}" />
  <tr class="prop">
      <td valign="top" class="name">
          <label>In Reply to:</label>
      </td>
      <td valign="top" class="value">
          ${messageInstance.parent.author}
      </td>
  </tr>
</g:if>
```

Inside a <*g:if*> block, we added an "In Reply to:" label and filled in the subject appropriately. We also added a hidden field to store the message.parent value so that it can be passed to the save action to complete the link between a reply and its parent.

It's difficult to do justice to this functionality in print, but we'll try. In Figure 7.3, on the following page, we can see our new ajaxList view with a message selected, and in Figure 7.4, on page 123, we can see the result of clicking the Reply button for that message. If you've done anything like this before in another Java web framework, you're probably as impressed as I am by how easy it was to do this. I've heard that this sense of awe and amazement wears off after a while. But I'm still waiting.

7.3 Display Message Threads with a Custom Tag

Now we need to add nesting to our message list in order to visualize the various threads in our forum. We'll do this with a custom GSP tag. If you've ever written custom JSP tags or JSF components, come out from under the table. It's not like that at all. But just to reassure you, before we get started on our custom tag, we'll take a brief look at what it takes (or more important perhaps, *doesn't* take) to create a GSP tag.

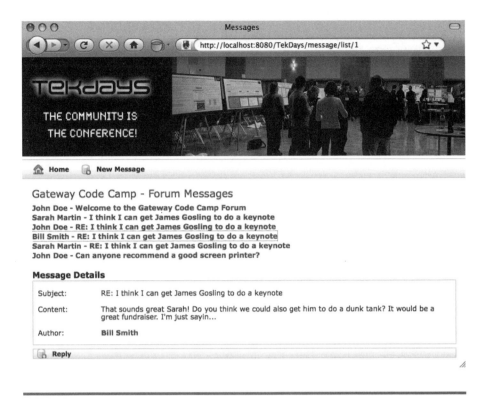

Figure 7.3: AJAX-ENABLED MESSAGE LIST

A Brief Introduction to GSP Tags

The first step is to create a TagLib. A TagLib is a Groovy class with a name ending in (surprise, surprise!) TagLib, and it lives in the grails-app/taglib directory. Grails provides a convenience script to create this for us:

```
$ grails create-tag-lib TekDays
```

This script will create TekDays/grails-app/taglib/TekDaysTagLib.groovy and a corresponding TestCase in TekDays/test/unit/TekDaysTagLibTests.groovy. In that one class, we can create as many GSP tags as we want, and they will automatically be available throughout our application. Each tag is a Groovy closure, with optional attrs and body parameters. For example:

```
def backwards = {attrs, body ->
    out << body().reverse()
}
```

This is a custom GSP tag that will reverse whatever text is contained in its body. So, <g:backwards>Hello</g:backwards> will render as olleH. That's not very useful but illustrative nonetheless. That's all there is

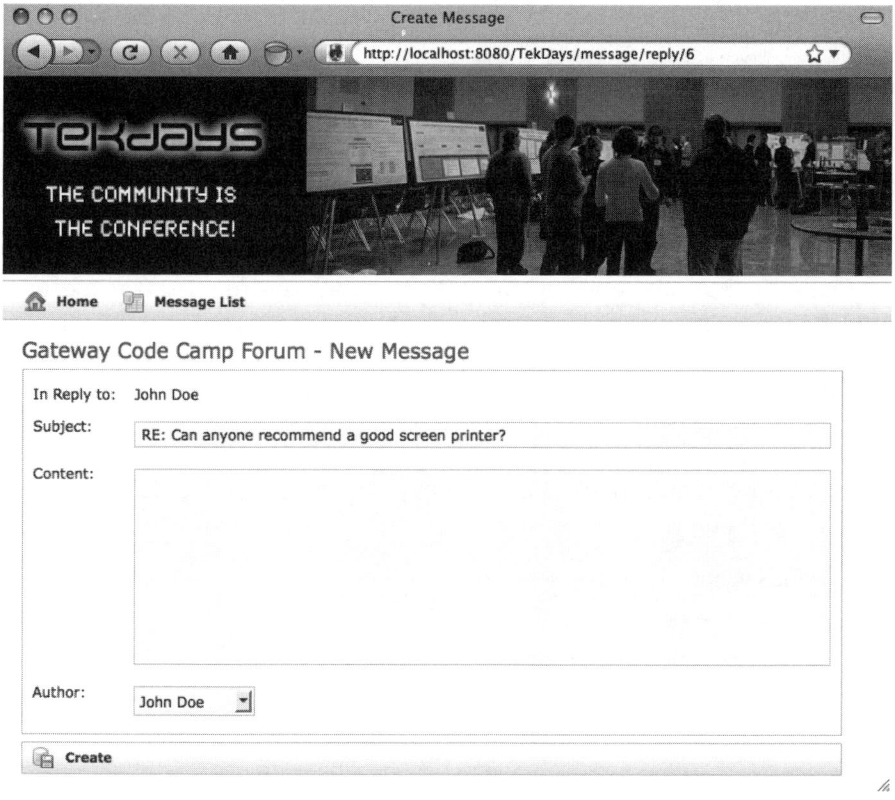

Figure 7.4: MESSAGE CREATE VIEW: REPLY

to it. There are no TLDs[3] to create, no config files to update, and no supporting classes or interfaces. A TagLib is just a Groovy class, and each tag is a closure with two optional parameters. The first parameter, which we call attrs, is a Map containing any attributes the tag needs. The second, referred to here as body, is a closure. The *names* given to these parameters are not important, but the *order* is. The attributes Map must always be the first parameter. Notice that our example did not use the attrs parameter, but it still needed to be there so that we could include the body.

It is so easy to create custom tags in Grails that there is no excuse not to. GSP tags can also be bundled into plug-ins to make it easier to

---

3. Tag library descriptor.

share them across projects or to make them available to the public—but that's a topic for another book.[4]

The MessageThread Tag

Our tag will be a bit more complex than the *<g:backward>* tag but not all that much more. We are currently using two tags to render our list of messages as links: the *<g:each>* tag handles the list traversal, and the *<g:remoteLink>* tag renders the link, with all the Ajax magic hidden inside. Our goal is to replace these with a single tag that will take a list of Message instances, create the same Ajax link for each one, and indent replies to provide the nested view of message threads.

If you haven't already, run the grails create-tag-lib script to create Tek-Days/grails-app/taglib/TekDaysTagLib.groovy, and then open that file. It will start looking like this:

`forum/TekDays/grails-app/taglib/TekDaysTagLib.groovy`

```
class TekDaysTagLib {

}
```

Add the following code, and then we'll go over what it's doing:

`forum.1/TekDays/grails-app/taglib/TekDaysTagLib.groovy`

```
class TekDaysTagLib {

  def messageThread = {attrs ->
    def messages = attrs.messages.findAll{msg -> !msg.parent}
    processMessages(messages, 0)
  }

  void processMessages(messages, indent){
    messages.each{msg ->

      def body = "${msg?.author} - ${msg?.subject}"
      out << "<div style='height:30; margin-left:${indent * 20};'>"
      out << "${remoteLink(action:'showDetail', id:msg.id, update:'details', body)}"
      out << "</div>"

      def children = Message.findAllByParent(msg)
      if (children){
          processMessages(children, indent + 1)
      }
    }
  }

}
```

---

4. *Grails in Action* has an excellent chapter on creating Grails plug-ins.

The first thing we have is our tag closure. It is declared just like a controller action, except for the attrs parameter. The tag closure has only two lines because we are moving most of the processing to a method called processMessages().

The tag code's main responsibility is preparing the starting point for the recursive process that is required to get the nesting we are after. To do this, we filter the list that is being passed in the messages attribute, using the findAll method that Groovy adds to Collection. This method will pass each element of a collection to the closure that it takes as a parameter. It will accept or reject the element based on the Boolean result of the closure. We are checking for the existence of a parent property in the Message. The existence of a value evaluates to true in Groovy, so we can shorten a statement like msg.parent == null to !msg.parent. The end result of this line is that we have a collection of *top-level* messages.

The next line passes our filtered collection, along with the number 0, to the processMessages() method. This method takes a collection of messages and an indent value; the first time it's called by the tag, it is given a collection of top-level messages and the number 0. We use the each() method to iterate over the messages. Instead of using the default it parameter for each(), we are explicitly declaring a msg parameter. msg, then, is a variable that represents each individual message.

Next, we define a body, made up of the message's author and its subject, for our link. Then we begin writing out to the response. The first thing we send to out is a *<div>*, which will help us with positioning our links; notice that we use the indent parameter to determine the amount of left-margin to apply. We next send the *<remoteLink>* tag to out. There is no multipass resolution of GSPs, so we can't write out other tags from our tag, but we *can* call other tags from our tag and write out the same result that they would have written. That's what we are doing here.

Recall that any GSP tag can be called as a method. The tag name becomes a method name, and the attributes become named parameters. If there is a body, it becomes the last parameter. (Notice that we have action:'showDetail' instead of action="showDetail".) Finally, we close the *<div>*. As each message in the collection is processed, these lines will be written out, and then we will perform a check to see whether that message has any replies.

We define a children variable, which we load with a call to Message.findAll-ByParent(). If the message we are working on has any replies, they will be in this collection. We then pass this collection to the processMessages()

method recursively, with the indent parameter incremented by 1. This will cause each new level of replies to be indented another 20 pixels and will ensure that all replies are accounted for, no matter how deeply they may be nested.

Having this logic in the page would have been a mess, and it would have been unbearably cumbersome to do it in the controller. A custom tag is the perfect solution to this problem. Indeed, GSP custom tags are the perfect solution to many of the UI problems faced by web developers; that's why they are my second favorite Grails feature (the first favorite is GORM, since I am a recovering EJB developer). GSP tags are also a great way to reuse view code and keep your pages DRY.

Not only does this tag prevent us from adding more code to our page, it also allows us to remove some. Let's open TekDays/grails-app/views/message/ajaxList.gsp and replace the five lines encompassing the <*g:each*> tag with the following single line:

```
forum.1/TekDays/grails-app/views/message/ajaxList.gsp
```

```
<div id="messageList">
  <g:messageThread messages="${messageInstanceList}" />
</div>
```

In Figure 7.5, on the facing page, we can see what our handiwork looks like. Not bad.

7.4 Summary

Wow! This was a very productive iteration. We implemented one of the most critical features of our application; a community-based event-organizing effort is doomed without good communication. While we were at it, we learned about three important features of Grails. Grails templates are a convenient way of sharing common portions of GSP code and are very helpful when using Ajax. We also learned that Grails makes working with Ajax a snap, while not locking you into any one JavaScript library. Then we got an overview and some good practice with those awesome custom GSP tags.

We'll be moving into security and related issues next, but now it's time for a short break. It's time to catch up on the latest issue of GroovyMag[5] to see what's new in this thriving community.

---

5. A monthly e-magazine devoted to Groovy, Grails, and Griffon: http://groovymag.com.

Figure 7.5: THREADED MESSAGE LIST

Chapter 8

Knock, Knock: Who's There? Grails Security

Our customer keeps asking me when we are going to add security. I keep telling him, "As soon as we need it." We were just getting into a lively debate when my wife started giving me funny looks. But seriously, as we progress with the TekDays application, it's going to be very helpful to know who's using the application. Not only would that allow us to limit access to certain data or areas of the application, but it would also let us be more intelligent about what we display to users.

Our goal this time around is to implement a simple security system and see how we can use it to provide a more customized user experience.

8.1 Grails Security Options

Grails provides several options when it comes to security, from rolling your own with *controller interceptors* and *filters* to using plug-ins for the more popular Java security frameworks out there. As of this writing, the main Grails plug-in repository has seventeen security-related plug-ins.

There are plug-ins for JSecurity, CAS, Spring Security (two of them), Atlassian Crowd, and more. There is also the simple yet effective Authentication plug-in, which doesn't rely on any external libraries. There are plug-ins for Captchas, an OpenID plug-in...you get the picture. For your *next* Grails application, it would be wise to spend some time looking at these plug-ins to see whether one or more of them might meet your needs.[1] For this project, however, we are going to implement our own solution using Grails filters.

8.2 Logging In

Before we get into creating filters and building our security system, let's talk about what we want the system to do. First, we want to know who is currently using the system; that is, are they an anonymous user (which is fine), or are they represented by a TekUser instance? Next, we want to restrict access to certain areas of the application based on the current user. For example, only organizers should be able to edit a TekEvent instance, and only organizers *or* volunteers should be able to participate in the event's forum.

For the first step, we will need some sort of login process. We will create two new actions in the TekUserController: login and logout. Then we will create a new login view.

Open TekDays/grails-app/controllers/TekUserController.groovy, and add the following action:

```
def login = {

}
```

Interestingly, we don't need anything in this action; simply having an action with that name will cause the GSP that we are about to create to be rendered. Let's create TekDays/grails-app/views/tekUser/login.gsp and give it the following code:

security/TekDays/grails-app/views/tekUser/login.gsp

```html
<html>
  <head>
    <meta http-equiv="Content-Type" content="text/html; charset=UTF-8"/>
    <meta name="layout" content="main" />
    <title>Login</title>
  </head>
  <body>
    <g:if test="${flash.message}">
    <div class="message">${flash.message}</div>
    </g:if>
    <g:form action="validate">
      <table>
        <tr class="prop">
```

---

1. http://grails.org/plugins

```
          <td class="name">
            <label for="username">User Name:</label>
          </td>
          <td class="value">
            <input type="text" id="username" name="username" value="">
          </td>
        </tr>
        <tr class="prop">
          <td class="name">
            <label for="password">Password:</label>
          </td>
          <td class="value">
            <input type="password" id="password" name="password" value="">
          </td>
        </tr>
        <tr>
          <td></td>
          <td><input type="submit" value="login"/></td>
        </tr>
      </table>
    </g:form>
  </body>
</html>
```

Simple enough. After the standard Grails message block (which we will need if there are problems during login), we have an HTML form with fields for username and password, followed by a submit button. This page will be merged with our standard header because of this line: <meta name="layout" content="main" />. The final result can be seen in Figure 8.1, on the next page.

One important point about this code is the action that we've assigned to the <g:form>: validate. This action will be called when we submit the form. It will reside in the TekUserController and will use the form data to load an existing TekUser if found. We'll create this action now. Open TekDays/grails-app/controllers/TekUserController.groovy, and add the following action:

```
def validate = {
    def user = TekUser.findByUserName(params.username)
    if (user && user.password == params.password){
        session.user = user
        redirect(controller:'tekEvent', action:'list')
    }
    else{
      flash.message = "Invalid username and password."
      render(view:'login')
    }
}
```

Figure 8.1: THE LOGIN PAGE

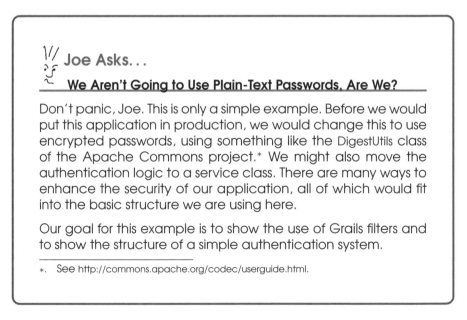

〜 Joe Asks. . .

We Aren't Going to Use Plain-Text Passwords, Are We?

Don't panic, Joe. This is only a simple example. Before we would put this application in production, we would change this to use encrypted passwords, using something like the DigestUtils class of the Apache Commons project.* We might also move the authentication logic to a service class. There are many ways to enhance the security of our application, all of which would fit into the basic structure we are using here.

Our goal for this example is to show the use of Grails filters and to show the structure of a simple authentication system.

∗. See http://commons.apache.org/codec/userguide.html.

This action, rather than the login action, does the real work of logging a user into the system. In the first line, we define the variable user to which we assign the result of a call to TekUser.findByUserName(params. username). Next we check to see whether our user has a value and, if so, whether its password matches params.password. If both of those things are true, then we'll stuff this TekUser instance in the session for later use and call the redirect() method to send the user to the list action of the TekEvent controller. If either is false, we add a message to flash and call the render() method to redisplay the login view.

You'll notice that we used two methods that we didn't define anywhere. The redirect() and render() are added to all controller classes at runtime by Grails. The redirect() method will perform an HTTP redirect. That is, it will return a response to the client that will cause it to make a subsequent call to the URL that is created by the controller and action parameters.

The render() method is very versatile. We used it earlier to respond to an Ajax call. In that instance, we passed it a *template*; here we pass it a *view*. In both cases, the end result was to send a chunk of text back to the client. This method can also be used to render XML, JSON, or any arbitrary text to the client.

In this action, we write to session, which is a Map stored in the *Session* scope. Anything we put there will be available as long as this user is interacting with our application. And since it is a Groovy Map, we can add new key/value pairs by assigning a value to a nonexistent key. There was no user key in session, but we added the key and assigned the value in the following line: session.user = user. We did the same with flash, which is a Map stored in a special scope that lasts for this request and the next, after which the values we put in will be cleared out.

Now that we have a login page and a process for logging a user in, let's see how we can use filters to prompt the user to login at the appropriate times.

8.3   Filters

Filters allow us to hook into, or intercept, the processing of a request. There are interceptors for before, after, and afterView. There are many uses for filters, and you can have as many filters as you need in an application. In our case, we'll use a filter to determine whether a user is logged in when they try to access a "secure" page.

I know this must be sounding like a broken record (does anyone remember what that is?), but Grails makes implementing filters a snap. Create a Groovy class with a name ending in *Filters*, and place it in the grails-app/conf directory. In this class, define a code block called filters, and then include individual filters as if they were methods. Each filter (method) can take named parameters for controller and action. Calls to this controller and action pair will be intercepted by this filter. (An asterisk can be used as a wildcard to represent any controller or action.) But enough chatter—let's get to the code.

Create a new file called TekDays/grails-app/conf/SecurityFilters.groovy. Open this file, and add the following code:

```
security/TekDays/grails-app/conf/SecurityFilters.groovy
```

```groovy
class SecurityFilters {
  def filters = {
    doLogin(controller:'*', action:'*'){
        before = {
              if (!controllerName)
                 return true
            def allowedActions = ['show', 'index', 'list', 'login', 'validate']
            if (!session.user && !allowedActions.contains(actionName)){
              redirect(controller:'tekUser', action:'login',
                    params:['cName': controllerName, 'aName':actionName])
              return false
            }
        }
    }
  }
}
```

In our SecurityFilters class, we create a single filter called doLogin with a before interceptor. We use wildcards for both controller and action parameters, which means this filter will be called for all actions. We don't actually want to require the user to log in for every action, so we will fine-tune this filter further.

Every filter has certain properties injected into it by Grails; among these are controllerName and actionName. These represent the original controller and action that the user was trying to access before the filter so rudely interrupted. We will use the actionName to determine whether we really want to filter this call. We'll do this in two steps. In the first step, we'll check to see whether we have a controllerName. If we don't, then we can assume the user is going to the default home page (index.gsp), in which case we will return true. For the second step, we define a List variable with the names of actions that we want to *allow*. Along with the innocuous actions like show and list, we included the login and validate actions to avoid unintended login loops. Then in our **if** comparison, we check to see whether this list contains the current actionName.

The other thing we check in the **if** comparison is whether we already have a user in the session. If we do not have a user and the current action is not in the allowedActions list, we redirect to the login action of the TekUserController and pass along the controllerName and actionName values in the params parameter. (We'll need them shortly.) In the final line, we return false, which will prevent any other filters (or the original action) from being called.

Now to make this all work nicely, we have to go back and make a few changes to our login view and the two controller actions we added to TekUserController. We want to take advantage of the controllerName and actionName values from the filter. When the filter redirects to the login action, it will pass these values in the params, so we need to do something with them to keep them available. Open TekDays/grails-app/controllers/TekUserController.groovy, and modify the empty login action like so:

security/TekDays/grails-app/controllers/TekUserController.groovy

```
def login = {
    if (params.cName)
        return [cName:params.cName, aName:params.aName]
}
```

This code checks to see whether those two values are available in params and, if so, passes them on to the view in the returned Map. Next, we'll modify the view to pass these values on to the validate action. Open TekDays/grails-app/views/tekUser/login.gsp, and add the following hidden input elements somewhere inside the <*g:form*>.

security/TekDays/grails-app/views/tekUser/login.gsp

```
<input type="hidden" name="cName" value="${cName}">
<input type="hidden" name="aName" value="${aName}">
```

Now when the form is submitted, the controllerName and actionName values from the filter will be passed on to the validate action. We will now use these values to redirect the user to their original destination on successful login.

Open TekDays/grails-app/controllers/TekUserController.groovy, and modify the validate action to look like this:

security/TekDays/grails-app/controllers/TekUserController.groovy

```
def validate = {
    def user = TekUser.findByUserName(params.username)
    if (user && user.password == params.password){
        session.user = user
        if (params.cName)
            redirect(controller:params.cName, action:params.aName)
        else
            redirect(controller:'tekEvent', action:'list')
    }
    else{
      flash.message = "Invalid username and password."
      render(view:'login')
    }
}
```

What we're doing here is checking to see whether the controllerName and actionName (using shortened variables) are available. If they are, we use them to redirect the user; otherwise, we redirect them to the list action of the TekEvent as before. We can come back and change that to the *home* page later (after we add one).

This feature is a bit tricky to show in screenshots, but go ahead and try it. Run the application, and go to the default home page. Choose any of the controller links, and you should come to the list view. Click the New button, and you should see the login screen shown in Figure 8.1, on page 132. Log in using the credentials of one of the users we created earlier, and you should be redirected to the create view that you were aiming at. Good deal!

8.4 Logging Out

Since we have a method for logging in and because I like—er, I mean our customer is quite fond of symmetry, we should add a method for logging out. Don't worry, it'll take only a couple lines of code. Go back to TekDays/grails-app/controllers/TekUserController, and add a logout action, like so:

security/TekDays/grails-app/controllers/TekUserController.groovy

```
def logout = {
    session.user = null
    redirect(url:resource(dir:''))
}
```

Since the way that our filter determines whether a user is logged in is by the existence of a value in the user key, we set that key to null to "log them out." We don't need to check for a user key before we do this; if it doesn't exist, it will be created and set to null. Then we redirect to a URL that we create with the help of the <*resource*> tag. (Recall that all GSP tags can be called as methods.) This will send the logged-out user back to the home page.

Now we can log in and out of the system, but the only way we can do either directly is to type the appropriate URL into our browser (for example, http://localhost:8080/TekDays/tekUser/login). That's not very Web 2.0. It's more like Web 0.5. What would be great is if we had a login/logout toggle that we could display where appropriate. Sounds like a great place for a custom tag.

Go back to our taglib at TekDays/grails-app/taglib/TekDaysTagLib.groovy and add a new tag closure called loginToggle:

```
security/TekDays/grails-app/taglib/TekDaysTagLib.groovy
def loginToggle = {
  out << "<div>"
  if (session.user){
    out << "<span style='float:left'>"
    out << "Welcome ${session.user}."
    out << "</span><span style='float:right;margin-right:10px'>"
    out << "<a href='${createLink(controller:'tekUser', action:'logout')}'>"
    out << "Logout </a></span>"
  }
  else{
    out << "<span style='float:right;margin-right:10px'>"
    out << "<a href='${createLink(controller:'tekUser', action:'login')}'>"
    out << "Login </a></span>"
  }
  out << "</div><br/>"
}
```

This tag doesn't need any attributes or a body, so we skip the closure parameters altogether. We start by writing out an opening <*div*>. Then we check to see whether a user exists. If we have a user, we output a "Welcome" message and a link to allow them to log out. For the message, we use ${session.user} inside a GString. (This will lead to a call to the TekUser.toString() method, which we defined earlier.) For the link we use a regular anchor tag along with the <*createLink*> tag, called as a method. If there is no user, we just output a link to allow the user to log in. There's also a little CSS, but that's not too exciting.

Figure 8.2: The LOGINTOGGLE TAG IN ACTION

We'll use this new tag in TekDays/grails-app/views/layouts/main.gsp, so go ahead and open that file. Add the <g:loginToggle> tag, as shown here:

security/TekDays/grails-app/views/layouts/main.gsp

```
<div class="logo">
  <img src="${resource(dir:'images',file:'td_logo.png')}" alt="TekDays"/>
  <g:loginToggle />
</div>
```

We can see how our new custom tag looks in Figure 8.2. Much better.

8.5 Summary

That went quickly! It's OK—you can use the extra time to do a little experimenting. Maybe you can try using filters to add logging or something exciting like that. We now have the beginnings of a workable security system in place for TekDays. It's not as robust as those provided by the Spring Security or JSecurity plug-ins, but it'll work for our purposes. We also have a new custom tag in our growing tag library.

Next up, we'll start tying some of these pieces together with a more useful home page and a dashboard view for event organizers. We'll see how Grails allows us to build much more than single-domain views and that MVC doesn't have to be a collection of silos. It just keeps getting better!

Chapter 9

Big-Picture Views

So far, the views we've been building have been focused on a single domain class. The Grails convention-based MVC architecture allows us to build these types of views quickly, and they play an important role in most applications. But most applications—TekDays included—will also need a way to interact with data from multiple domain classes at a time.

The person taking on the responsibility of organizing a community technical event has a big job on their hands; it's an exciting and rewarding job, but a big one nonetheless. We're here to help that hard-working, visionary individual, and one way we can do that is to provide a more convenient way for them to see details about their event and to perform common tasks. In this iteration, we're going to implement an organizer's dashboard view. This view will not be tied to any one domain class but will interact with most (if not all) of them at one time. We might even hit data that is not from our domain.

Before we launch into what will arguably be the most complex view of our application, let's warm up with another view that needs some work. Our home page could really use some love. The list of controller links is getting kind of old, so let's warm up our GSP muscles with a home page makeover.

9.1 Home Page Makeover

The application home page can be found in the root views directory: TekDays/grails-app/views/index.gsp.

Let's open this file now to see what we have to work with:

`security/TekDays/grails-app/views/index.gsp`

```
<html>
  <head>
    <title>Welcome to Grails</title>
        <meta name="layout" content="main" />
  </head>
  <body>
    <h1 style="margin-left:20px;">Welcome to Grails</h1>
    <p style="margin-left:20px;width:80%">
      Congratulations, you have successfully started your first Grails application!
       At the moment this is the default page, feel free to modify it to either
       redirect to a controller or display whatever content you may choose. Below
       is a list of controllers that are currently deployed in this application,
       click on each to execute its default action:
    </p>
    <div class="dialog" style="margin-left:20px; width:60%;">
      <ul>
        <g:each var="c" in="${grailsApplication.controllerClasses}">
          <li class="controller">
            <g:link controller="${c.logicalPropertyName}">${c.fullName}</g:link>
          </li>
        </g:each>
      </ul>
    </div>
  </body>
</html>
```

We'll be getting rid of most of this, but it is interesting to see what's going on here. The <g:each> tag is iterating over a list of all the controllers in the application and creating a link for each one. Looking at things like grailsApplication.controllerClasses gives you an idea of the types of things you can do with Grails as you move on from here. Grails is by no means a shallow framework!

As interesting as that code is, it doesn't do what we need right now, so we'll get rid of everything in the <body> section. Then in the <head>, we'll change the <title> to the name and slogan of our application. We'll replace the <body> with a welcome paragraph and a few <div> blocks to represent the major tasks in TekDays. The end result should look like this:

`bigger/TekDays/grails-app/views/index.gsp`

```
<html>
  <head>
    <title>TekDays - The Community is the Conference!</title>
        <meta name="layout" content="main" />
  </head>
```

Figure 9.1: THE TEKDAYS HOME PAGE

```
<body>
  <div id="welcome">
    <h3>Welcome to TekDays.com</h3>
    <p>TekDays.com is a site dedicated to assisting individuals and communities
       to organize technology conferences.  To bring great minds with common
       interests and passions together for the good of greater geekdom!
    </p>
  </div>
  <div class="homeCell">
    <h3>Find a Tek Event</h3>
    <p>
      See if there's a technical event in the works that strikes your fancy.
      If there is, you can volunteer to help or just let the organizers know
      that you'd be interested in attending.  Everybody has a role to play.
    </p>
      <span class="buttons" >
        <g:link controller="tekEvent" action="list">Find a Tek Event</g:link>
      </span>
  </div>
```

```
        <div class="homeCell">
          <h3>Organize a Tek Event</h3>
          <p>
            If you don't see anything that suits your interest and location, then
            why not get the ball rolling.  It's easy to get started and there may
            be others out there ready to get behind you to make it happen.
          </p>
            <span class="buttons" >
              <g:link controller="tekEvent" action="create">
                Organize a Tek Event
              </g:link>
            </span>
        </div>
        <div class="homeCell">
          <h3>Sponsor a Tek Event</h3>
          <p>
            If you are part of a business or organization that is involved in
            technology then sponsoring a tek event would be a great way to let the
            community know that you're there and you're involved.
          </p>
            <span class="buttons" >
              <g:link controller="sponsor" action="create">
                Sponsor a Tek Event
              </g:link>
            </span>
        </div>
      </body>
</html>
```

That's kind of a long listing, but it's not very complicated. We broke the page up into four blocks: an introduction and one section each for the three main activities users will do in our application. There are other activities, but they will be branches off of these three—browsing events, creating an event, or becoming a sponsor.

In Figure 9.1, on the preceding page, we can see our new home page in all its glory (so to speak).

9.2 Creating a New Controller

Now that we're all warmed up and ready, we'll get to work on the new organizer's dashboard view. To keep our overall architecture clean and not confuse the conventions that have proved so helpful to us, we will create a new controller for the dashboard view and any related views. We'll use the create-controller script to do this:

```
$ grails create-controller Dashboard
```

Controllers and Conventions

The Grails convention of naming a controller with a domain class name followed by *Controller*, and the way that the generate-all script takes a domain class and generates a conventionally named controller and standard views in a directory with the same name, can make it seem like everything must be based on a domain class. The fact is that aside from the work of generate-all, there is no link between a domain class and a controller.

Any domain class can be accessed from any controller. The static methods that Grails adds to domain classes (get(), list(), and so on) are available in any controller.

The real convention-based link is between controllers and *views*. An action in a controller will, unless directed otherwise, attempt to render a view named after the action, in a directory named after the controller. For example, a bar action in FooController will attempt to render the view in ../grails-app/views/foo/bar.gsp.

The script creates the file TekDays/grails-app/controllers/DashboardController.groovy, along with a corresponding TestCase in TekDays/test/unit/DashboardControllerTests.groovy. It also creates the TekDays/grails-app/views/dashboard directory, where our new controller will look for views.

This controller will be responsible for rendering the dashboard view and supplying it with the necessary data. To be clearer about what data we need, we'll work on the view first. Once we have that done, we'll come back to the DashboardController.

9.3 Designing the Dashboard View

The purpose of the dashboard view is to give event organizers and volunteers an "at-a-glance" view of the most pertinent information regarding their event, with links to get to where they need to go. This will be their starting place when they come to work on their event.

We'll discuss the design more as we go along, but to get started, create an empty file called TekDays/grails-app/views/dashboard/dashboard.gsp, and add the following code:

bigger/TekDays/grails-app/views/dashboard/dashboard.gsp

```
<html>
  <head>
    <title>TekDays - Dashboard</title>
    <meta name="layout" content="main" />
  </head>
  <body>
  </body>
</html>
```

This page will have a good amount of content in it, so in order to keep it manageable from a coding standpoint, we'll compose the page out of a series of templates. Our main dashboard page will consist of several <g:render> tags, which can easily be rearranged and styled as necessary. We'll add these tags now and then create the templates they refer to. In dashboard.gsp, add the following code between the opening and closing <body> tags:

bigger/TekDays/grails-app/views/dashboard/dashboard.gsp

```
<div id="event" style='margin:10px 10px 10px 10px'>
  <g:render template="event" model="${['event':event]}" />
</div>
<div id="tasks" style='margin:10px 10px 10px 10px'>
  <g:render template="tasks" model="${['tasks':tasks]}" />
</div>
<div id="volunteers" style='margin:10px 10px 10px 10px'>
  <g:render template="volunteers" model="${['volunteers':volunteers]}" />
</div>
<div id="messages" style='margin:10px 10px 10px 10px'>
  <g:render template="messages" model="${[messages:messages]}" />
</div>
<div id="sponsors" style='margin:10px 10px 10px 10px'>
  <g:render template="sponsors" model="${[sponsorships:sponsorships]}" />
</div>
```

We added several <div> tags containing <g:render> tags. We can tweak the styling on these elements or change their order or what have you. Now we can address each template on its own, which will help our discussion (as well as our code) to be more organized. Recall that the <g:render> tag will insert the final HTML of the designated template inside the containing element, in this case the <div>. Let's start with the template for the basic event information.

Basic Event Information

In this first template we'll have information from the TekEvent itself, such as name, city, dates, and venue. We'll display the event name and city at the top center and then build a simple table to display the other data elements. Create the file TekDays/grails-app/views/dashboard/_event.gsp, and give it the following code:

bigger/TekDays/grails-app/views/dashboard/_event.gsp

```
<span style="text-align:center">
  <h1>${event}</h1>
</span>
<table>
  <tr>
    <td>
      Start Date: <g:formatDate format="MMM/dd/yyyy" date="${event.startDate}"/>
    </td>
    <td>
      <g:if test="${event.endDate}">
        End Date: <g:formatDate format="MMM/dd/yyyy" date="${event.endDate}"/>
      </g:if>
    </td>
  </tr>
  <tr>
    <td>
      Venue: ${event.venue}
    </td>
    <td>
      Number of potential attendees: ${event.respondents.size()}
    </td>
  </tr>
</table>
```

Notice that we also displayed the number of potential attendees. This is not a data element itself but is the count of the respondents collection property. This is the type of information that we will want at a glance; the complete list of respondents' email addresses would be overkill here.

Tasks

Next up is the task list. This will be an abbreviated list of the first five incomplete tasks, with a link to go to the full task list.

Create TekDays/grails-app/views/dashboard/_tasks.gsp, and add this code:

bigger/TekDays/grails-app/views/dashboard/_tasks.gsp

```
<h3>Things to do</h3>
<table>
  <thead>
    <tr>
      <th>Task Title</th>
      <th>Due Date</th>
      <th>Assigned To</th>
    </tr>
  </thead>
  <g:each in="${tasks}" var="task">
    <tr>
      <td>${task.title}</td>
      <td><g:formatDate format="MM/dd/yyyy" date="${task.dueDate}" /></td>
      <td>${task.assignedTo}</td>
    </tr>
  </g:each>
</table>
<g:link controller="task" action="list" id="${event.id}">
  View all ${event.tasks.size()} tasks for this event.
</g:link>
```

The template starts out with a heading, followed by a table with three columns displaying the title, dueDate, and assignedTo properties of each Task. Then we finish off with a link to the rest of the tasks for this event. (Notice that we take advantage of the GSP being one big GString by embedding a Groovy expression in the middle of the <*g:link*> body.)

Volunteers

For the volunteers template, create TekDays/grails-app/views/dashboard/ _volunteers.gsp, and enter the following code:

bigger/TekDays/grails-app/views/dashboard/_volunteers.gsp

```
<h3>Volunteers</h3>
<table>
  <thead>
    <tr>
      <th>Name</th>
      <th>Email Address</th>
      <th>Web Site</th>
    </tr>
  </thead>
  <g:each in="${volunteers}" var="volunteer">
    <tr>
      <td>
        <g:link controller="tekUser" action="show" id="${volunteer.id}">
          ${volunteer.fullName}
        </g:link>
      </td>
```

```
      <td><a href="mailto:${volunteer.email}">${volunteer.email}</a></td>
      <td><a href="http://${volunteer.website}">${volunteer.website}</a></td>
    </tr>
  </g:each>
</table>
```

The volunteers template starts out the same as the tasks template with a header, a table with three columns, and a row for each volunteer. One difference is that we are not limiting the list of volunteers; the whole gang will be there. Some other differences are the links that we are building in. Notice the <g:link> tag that we use inside the full-Name<td>. This will create a link to the show action of the TekUser controller with the id of the given volunteer. We also used HTML anchor tags to turn the volunteer's email and website into links. Now the organizer has a quick way to fire off an email to a volunteer.

Messages

Next, we'll have a top-level list of the messages in the forum. Create a blank file called TekDays/grails-app/views/dashboard/_messages.gsp, and code it as follows:

bigger/TekDays/grails-app/views/dashboard/_messages.gsp

```
<h3>Forum Messages</h3>
<table>
  <thead>
    <tr>
      <th>Author</th>
      <th>Subject</th>
      <th>Content</th>
    </tr>
  </thead>
  <g:each in="${messages}" var="msg">
    <tr>
      <td>
        <g:link controller="tekUser" action="show" id="${msg.author.id}">
          ${msg.author}
        </g:link>
      </td>
      <td>${msg.subject}</td>
      <td>
        ${msg.content[0..Math.min(msg.content.size() -1, 24)]}
        ${msg.content.size() > 25 ? '...' : ''}
      </td>
    </tr>
  </g:each>
</table>
<g:link controller="message" action="list" id="${event.id}">
  View threaded messages for this event.
</g:link>
```

This code is similar to the others: a table with three columns and a
<g:each> tag to iterate over the messages and fill the table. The mes-
sages list will contain only top-level messages (no replies), but this will
be handled in the controller. One interesting thing that we did in this
template is truncate the content if it is more than 25 characters long.

Groovy allows us to retrieve a portion of a String using a *range*, as in the
following example:

```
def s = 'Grails is fun!'
assert s[0..5] == 'Grails'
```

In our template, this line:

```
${msg.content[0..Math.min(msg.content.size() -1, 24)]}
```

uses a *range* to get the first 25 characters of the content property of the
message. To avoid getting an IndexOutOfBounds exception if the content
is shorter than 25 characters, we used Math.min(). In the next line:

```
${msg.content.size() > 25 ? '...' : ''}
```

we tacked on an ellipsis, using a Java *ternary* operator. If we were going
to do this anywhere else, it would be another good candidate for a custom tag.

Sponsors

This last template will contain a Sponsor list. But as we discussed in
Section 4.6, *Many-to-Many Relationships*, on page 58, the TekEvent has
no direct relationship with the Sponsor class; we have to work with the
intermediate class Sponsorship. (Our template will actually contain information from both Sponsor and Sponsorship.) Create a blank file called
TekDays/grails-app/views/dashboard/_sponsors.gsp, and add the following
code:

```
<h3>Sponsors</h3>
<table>
  <thead>
    <tr>
      <th>Name</th>
      <th>Web Site</th>
      <th>Contribution</th>
    </tr>
  </thead>
```

```
<g:each in="${sponsorships}" var="s">
  <tr>
    <td>
      <g:link controller="sponsor" action="show" id="${s.sponsor.id}">
        ${s.sponsor.name}
      </g:link>
    </td>
    <td><a href="http://${s.sponsor.website}">${s.sponsor.website}</a></td>
    <td>${s.contributionType}</td>
  </tr>
</g:each>
</table>
```

The <g:each> tag in this template is iterating over a list of Sponsorship instances. Each instance is being stored in the variable s. To get the sponsor.name and sponsor.website properties, we accessed the sponsor property of the Sponsorship class like this: ${s.sponsor.name}. The contributionType is a property of the Sponsorship class, so we can access it directly. We also implemented links to the Sponsor show view and the sponsor's website, the same way we did for the volunteers template.

Now we have the basic components of our dashboard page. We will come back to it later and add some features to make it more useful, but first we want to close the feedback loop and see this view in action. To do that, we need to add the controller action that will collect the data we need and serve up the view.

9.4 Adding the Dashboard Action

We can tell from looking at the code for our dashboard view that it will need the following data elements when it is rendered: event, tasks, volunteers, messages, and sponsorships. The first of these is a single TekEvent instance; the rest are collections of related objects.

Some of these collections need to be filtered or limited in some way. This will also be done in the controller action.

Let's see how easy this can be. Open TekDays/grails-app/controllers/DashboardController.groovy. The empty index action should already be there. Right after that, add the dashboard action, as shown on the next page.

bigger/TekDays/grails-app/controllers/DashboardController.groovy

```groovy
class DashboardController {

    def index = { }

    def dashboard = {
        def event = TekEvent.get(params.id)
        if (event){
            if(event.organizer.userName == session.user.userName ||
               event.volunteers.collect{it.userName}.contains(
                                          session.user.userName)){
                def tasks = Task.findAllByEventAndCompleted(event, false,
                                          [max:5, sort:'dueDate'
                def volunteers = event.volunteers
                def messages = Message.findAllByEventAndParentIsNull(event,
                                                          [sort:'id',
                                                         order:'desc'
                def sponsorships = event.sponsorships
                return [event:event, tasks:tasks, volunteers:volunteers,
                        messages:messages, sponsorships:sponsorships]
            }
            else{
                flash.message = "Access to dashboard for ${event.name} denied."
                redirect(controller:'tekEvent', action:'list')
            }
        }
        else{
            flash.message = "No event was found with an id of ${params.id}"
            redirect(controller:'tekEvent', action:'list')
        }
    }
}
```

This action expects an id in the params Map. We first use that value to retrieve a TekEvent instance, using the TekEvent.get() method. The rest of the code is wrapped in a couple of **if** blocks. If the event is null, we add a message to flash and redirect the user to the TekEvent list. If the event is not null, then we check to see whether the logged-in user has access to this view.

This view is for event organizers or volunteers, so we check to see whether the logged-in user (session.user) is either the organizer or a user in the list of volunteers. Determining whether the logged-in user is the organizer is a simple comparison, but determining whether the logged-in user is among the volunteers is a bit tricky. We use the collect() method on event.volunteers to iterate over the Set and return a list containing the userName of each volunteer. Then we call the contains()

method on that list, passing in the userName of the logged-in user. If that test is passed, we begin retrieving the rest of the data.

The tasks variable is a list of Task instances associated with this TekEvent. We could use the tasks property of the TekEvent class, as we will do with others, but we want to limit the list to the first five incomplete tasks. Dynamic finders give us an easy way to do this. All the Grails dynamic finders allow a Map parameter, which can contain the following elements: offset, max, sort, and order. These values are used for pagination and sorting, which we get in the scaffolded list views, for example. We take advantage of max to limit our list to five items and use sort to get the tasks that are most urgent.

We don't need to do anything special with the volunteers list, so we just take the event.volunteers property. The messages list should show the most recent messages, so we use a dynamic finder again (this time using the IsNull comparator) and pass in parameters in the Map to do a descending sort on the id property.

The sponsorships list is also a simple one, so we just use the sponsorships property of the TekEvent. Once we've defined and loaded all of the data elements our dashboard view needs, we return them in the params Map.

Now, if we log in as the event organizer or a volunteer and navigate to http://localhost:8080/TekDays/dashboard/dashboard/1, we're greeted with the page shown in Figure 9.2, on the following page.

9.5 Adding a Menu

Our dashboard view gives event organizers and volunteers a good look at most aspects of their event, but it would be nice if they could take some actions from there, too. We'll add a menu to the dashboard to enable that. Open TekDays/grails-app/views/dashboard/dashboard.gsp, and add the following code to the top of the <body> section:

bigger/TekDays/grails-app/views/dashboard/dashboard.gsp

```
<div class="nav">
    <span class="menuButton">
      <a class="home" href="${resource(dir:'')}">Home</a>
    </span>
    <span class="menuButton">
      <g:link class="create" controller="task" action="create">
        Create Task
      </g:link>
    </span>
```

Figure 9.2: TEKDAYS ORGANIZER'S DASHBOARD

Figure 9.3: THE DASHBOARD MENU

```
    <span class="menuButton">
      <g:link class="create" controller="sponsorship" action="create">
        Add Sponsor
      </g:link>
    </span>
    <span class="menuButton">
      <g:link class="list" controller="sponsor" action="list">
        All Sponsors
      </g:link>
    </span>
</div>
```

This code is mostly borrowed from the scaffolded pages that Grails gave us. We kept the Home menu item and added items to create new tasks and sponsorships. We also added a menu item to list all sponsors. (This might be useful to see who else is interested in sponsoring technical events.) We are using the *<g:link>* and *<g:resource>* tags, which we discussed earlier. One interesting thing here is the CSS classes that we are using: home, create, and list. These classes are provided by Grails and can be found in TekDays/web-app/css/main.css.

In Figure 9.3, we can what our dashboard menu looks like.

9.6 Linking to the Dashboard

Now that we have a dashboard view, we need to provide an easy way to get to it. The TekEvent show view is a logical place to provide a link to the dashboard. Open TekDays/grails-app/views/tekEvent/show.gsp, and add the highlighted code to the "menu" *<div>* near the top of the file.

Figure 9.4: THE EVENT SHOW VIEW MENU

```
bigger/TekDays/grails-app/views/tekEvent/show.gsp
        <div class="nav">
          <span class="menuButton">
            <a class="home" href="${resource(dir:'')}">Home</a>
          </span>
          <span class="menuButton">
            <g:link class="list" action="list">TekEvent List</g:link>
          </span>
          <span class="menuButton">
            <g:link class="create" action="create">New TekEvent</g:link>
          </span>
▶         <span class="menuButton">
▶           <g:link class="list" controller="dashboard" action="dashboard"
▶                 id="${tekEventInstance.id}">Event Dashboard</g:link>
▶         </span>
        </div>
```

Again, we just copied the existing menu code and modified the *<g:link>*
tag to go to the dashboard action of the DashboardController. Notice that
the variable used to represent the TekEvent instance is tekEventInstance
instead of event as we have been using. When modifying an existing
view, we have to use the variable names that are passed to it by the
controller. (To find out what they are, we can just look at the controller
action.)

The new menu on the show view is shown in Figure 9.4.

9.7 Summary

We now have a convenient dashboard view to help event organizers and volunteers keep an eye on their event, and we have an easy way for them to get to it. We have security in place so that only authorized users can get to the dashboard. As a bonus, we have a much friendlier and more helpful home page. And while we got all that done, we learned how to create a controller that is not tied to a domain class and use it to populate and access views that span multiple domain classes. We also got some good practice working with GSP views and templates. (Our customer is impressed, too, and that's always a good thing.)

In the next iteration, we'll be looking for a good way to add search capabilities to TekDays. This will introduce us to more of the coolness that is GORM and to the Grails plug-in architecture.

Chapter 10

Seek, and You Shall Find

Any nontrivial application needs to have some sort of search mechanism. TekDays is no exception. In fact, our customer informed me of three different places where he wants us to incorporate some sort of search behavior. Well, actually he wanted more than that, but I had to take a stand against scope creep. For now, we will implement these three: first, when a user logs into TekDays, we will find any TekEvent that has them as the organizer; second, we will also find any TekEvent for which they are a volunteer (both of these will show up on the home page); and finally, we will have the traditional search feature where users can look for a TekEvent based on the properties of the event. As we implement these new features, we will describe three common ways of searching and finding objects with Grails.

10.1 Search Using Dynamic Finders

When an event organizer logs into TekDays, we should give them a direct link to the event, or events, that they are organizing—these folks are busy; we don't want to waste their time. Fortunately, this is very easy to do using Grails' dynamic finders, introduced in Section 4.2, *Introducing GORM*, on page 49.

Here's the plan. When the user logs in, we will find all the TekEvent instances that have this user assigned to the organizer property. We will then display links to the show view for each TekEvent on the home page.

The search part of this feature is pretty simple, but we have to decide just where to do it and how to display it. Let's have a brief design session to see what we can come up with. We want to show the organizer's events on the home page, but the home page, unlike most pages in a

Grails application, is not rendered from a controller action. That means that we can't pass the event list to it in a model (a Map). We could retrieve the list right from the page with code like this:

```
<g:each in="${TekEvent.findAllByOrganizer(session.user)}" var="event">
  <!-- code to display event here -->
</g:each>
```

There are a couple problems with this approach. First, we are putting more code in our page than we should. Second, we would want to do this only if we have a logged-in user, so we would have to wrap this code in something like this:

```
<g:if test="${session.user}">
  <!-- each loop and corresponding code goes here -->
</g:if>
```

This would work, but it's ugly. So, what would be a good way to load and display these events every time the page loads for a logged-in event organizer? If you said "custom tag," you get a gold star by your name. This is an excellent case for a custom tag. Let's open our tag library, TekDays/grails-app/taglib/TekDaysTagLib.groovy, and add the following code at the end of the class:

```
seek/TekDays/grails-app/taglib/TekDaysTagLib.groovy

def organizerEvents = {
  if (session.user){
    def events = TekEvent.findAllByOrganizer(session.user)
    if (events){
      out << "<div style='margin-left:25px; margin-top:25px; width:85%'>"
      out << "<h3>Events you are organizing:</h3>"
      out << "<ul>"
      events.each{
          out << "<li><a href='"
          out << "${createLink(controller:'tekEvent',action:'show',id:it.id)}'>"
          out << "${it}</a></li>"
      }
      out << "</ul>"
      out << "</div>"
    }
  }
}
```

We defined a closure called organizerEvents that creates a tag called <g:organizerEvents>. This closure takes no parameters, which means that our new tag will not have a body or any attributes. Inside the closure, the first thing we do is check to see whether there is a logged-in user. (Recall from Chapter 8, *Knock, Knock: Who's There? Grails Security*, on page 129, that we store the logged-in user in session.user.)

If we have a user, we use the dynamic finder TekEvent.findAllByOrganizer() to get a list of TekEvent instances. In the next line, we check to see whether that call returned anything. In Groovy, a collection reference evaluates to false if it is null or empty. The next few lines set up a *<div>* and an *<ul>*.

Next, we used the each() method to iterate over our list of events and create a *<li>* and an *<a>* for each event. Notice how we used ${it} for the body of the *<a>* tag; this will call the toString() on the TekEvent, which returns name and city properties. Finally, we close out the unordered list and the *<div>*.

Now we can retrieve the list of events and display them on our home page by adding a single line of code. In TekDays/grails-app/views/index.gsp, add the highlighted line:

`seek/TekDays/grails-app/views/index.gsp`

```
    <h3>Welcome to TekDays.com</h3>
    <p>TekDays.com is a site dedicated to assisting individuals and communities
        to organize technology conferences.  To bring great minds with common
        interests and passions together for the good of greater geekdom!
    </p>
</div>
<g:organizerEvents />
<div class="homeCell">
  <h3>Find a Tek Event</h3>
  <p>
    See if there's a technical event in the works that strikes your fancy.
    If there is, you can volunteer to help or just let the organizers know
    that you'd be interested in attending.  Everybody has a role to play.
  </p>
    <span class="buttons">
      <g:link controller="tekEvent" action="list">Find a Tek Event</g:link>
    </span>
</div>
```

Not only have we avoided putting a bunch of business logic in our page, but we also have a tag that can easily be reused in other pages as needed. I don't know about you, but I'll sure sleep better at night.

Now that we have this nifty feature, let's make one more change to make it easier to see it in action. Currently, the validate action of the TekUserController redirects users to the TekEventController.list action after a successful login. We want to change that to redirect to the home

page. Open TekDays/grails-app/controllers/TekUserController.groovy, and find
the line in the validate action that looks like this:

```
redirect(controller:'tekEvent', action:'list')
```

Change that to look like the following highlighted line:

seek/TekDays/grails-app/controllers/TekUserController.groovy

```
    def validate = {
        def user = TekUser.findByUserName(params.username)
        if (user && user.password == params.password){
            session.user = user
            if (params.cName)
                redirect(controller:params.cName, action:params.aName)
            else
                redirect(uri:'/')
        }
        else{
          flash.message = "Invalid username and password."
          render(view:'login')
        }
    }
```

In most cases, the redirect() method will take an action or a controller and
action pair. But it can also take a URL or, as in this case, a URI. Simply
redirecting to a URI of / will return to the home page no matter where
we are in the application. Pretty handy.

In Figure 10.1, on the next page, we can see what this looks like after
our friend John Doe started up a couple more events.

10.2 Hibernate Criteria Builder

Dynamic finders are great, and as you work with Grails, you will find
yourself using them again and again, but they can take you only so
far. Specifically, dynamic finders are limited to searching based on two
properties of a domain class, and they are limited to top-level properties
of the class—you cannot use dynamic finders to search relationships.

Our next search feature is to find TekEvent instances for which a logged-
in user has volunteered. Volunteers for an event are in the volunteers
collection, which is the result of a one-to-many relationship between
TekEvent and TekUser. To search relationships, we must turn to a different
tool in the Grails toolbox.

The Criteria Builder in Grails is a very powerful and flexible tool for
retrieving objects. It is based on the Hibernate Criteria API, so you can

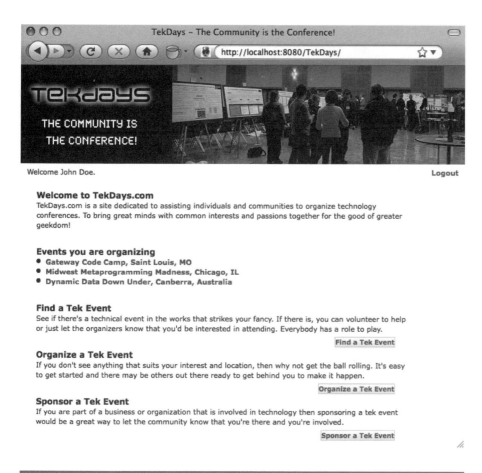

Figure 10.1: TEKDAYS HOME PAGE WITH ORGANIZER EVENTS

dig deeper by studying that technology.[1] However, this *is* Grails we're talking about, so you can do plenty with this tool by following some simple examples.

All Grails domain classes have a static createCriteria() method that returns a HibernateCriteriaBuilder instance. This builder has a list method that takes a closure. Inside this closure, we can define the criteria for our search.

---

1. https://www.hibernate.org/hib_docs/v3/api/org/hibernate/Criteria.html

Here's an example:

```
def g3Events = TekEvent.createCriteria.list{
  and{
    gt('startDate', new Date())
    or{
      ilike('description', '%groovy%')
      ilike('description', '%grails%')
      ilike('description', '%griffon%')
    }
  }
}
```

This code produces a list of the technical events that you would be likely to find me attending. More specifically, the g3Events list would contain any TekEvent that contained the words *Groovy*, *Grails*, or *Griffon* in the description property and whose startDate is still in the future. Notice how we have an or block nested inside an and block. This type of nesting of logical blocks can be much clearer and easier to read than an equivalent SQL statement.

Another nice feature of Criteria Builders is that relationship properties can easily be searched. This is also done with nested criteria blocks. Let's see how this looks:

```
def contegixEvents = TekEvent.createCriteria.list{
  sponsorships{
    sponsor{
      eq('name', 'Contegix')
    }
  }
}
```

This code loads contegixEvents with all TekEvent instances that Contegix is sponsoring. It does this by searching the sponsorships property, which is a collection of Sponsorship instances. That is represented by the first block. A Sponsorship has a sponsor property that is of type Sponsor. That's the second block. Then, within the sponsor block, we check for a name property that is equal to Contegix.

This last technique is the one we will use to find all events that a logged-in user has volunteered for. Since we want to display this list on the home page as we did for the organizer's event list, we will once again take advantage of Grails' custom tags. Let's open TekDays/grails-app/taglib/TekDaysTagLib.groovy and add the tag code at the top of the next page.

seek/TekDays/grails-app/taglib/TekDaysTagLib.groovy

```groovy
def volunteerEvents = {
  if (session.user){
    def events = TekEvent.createCriteria().list{
        volunteers{
          eq('id', session.user?.id)
        }
    }
    if (events){
      out << "<div style='margin-left:25px; margin-top:25px; width:85%'>"
      out << "<h3>Events you volunteered for:</h3>"
      out << "<ul>"
      events.each{
          out << "<li><a href='"
          out << "${createLink(controller:'tekEvent',action:'show',id:it.id)}'>"
          out << "${it}</a></li>"
      }
      out << "</ul>"
      out << "</div>"
    }
  }
}
```

Much of the code for our <g:volunteerEvents> tag is the same as the <g:organizerEvents> tag we created earlier. Let's take a look at the bits that are different. The most important difference is that we are using a Criteria Builder to load the events list. We are searching the volunteers collection for a TekUser with an id that is equal to the id of the logged-in user (session.user). The next difference is the heading, which isn't all that interesting. And finally, in this tag we are accessing the id of the session.user instead of the user by itself.

To put this new tag to use, open TekDays/grails-app/views/index.gsp, and add the highlighted line:

seek.1/TekDays/grails-app/views/index.gsp

```html
    <h3>Welcome to TekDays.com</h3>
    <p>TekDays.com is a site dedicated to assisting individuals and communities
        to organize technology conferences.  To bring great minds with common
        interests and passions together for the good of greater geekdom!
    </p>
  </div>
  <g:organizerEvents />
► <g:volunteerEvents />
```

Now when a user who has volunteered to help out with one or more events logs in, the home page will look similar to Figure 10.2, on the following page.

Figure 10.2: TEKDAYS HOME PAGE WITH VOLUNTEER EVENTS

10.3 The Big Guns: The Searchable Plug-In

So far, in this iteration we have implemented internal searches to add features for our users—and right nice features they are. But we're hoping that more people than just the organizer and the existing volunteers will access this site. We want to make it easy for visitors to find an event in their area or one related to their favorite technology. I know if I stumbled upon a site like this, the first thing I'd do is search for *Groovy* or *Grails*. Let's add this type of search feature to TekDays.

We could create a search form with fields for all the searchable properties, and then we could use the Criteria Builder to dynamically build a query based on the user's input—but that would be kind of lame. What we'll do instead is provide a single search field on our home page, and we'll search for all possible matches to the value entered in that field. To do this, we'll take advantage of one of the most powerful plug-ins in the Grails ecosystem; the Searchable plug-in[2] takes the indexing and search capabilities of Compass and Lucene and makes them easy to use. It makes them so easy, in fact, that we call it "Grails-easy."

Before we dig into this feature, let's talk about Grails' plug-ins. At last check, there are more than 200 plug-ins in the main repository. You can see what plug-ins are available by running grails list-plugins, and you can find the documentation for most of them at the main plug-in portal: http://grails.org/plugin/home. Installing a plug-in is as easy as running grails install-plugin plugin-name.

Plug-ins seamlessly add features to a Grails application. They can add new domain classes, controllers, tag libraries, services, and more. Often, plug-ins wrap an existing Java library or framework like the Twitter plug-in,[3] which wraps the JTwitter API.[4]

It's important to note that any library or framework that is provided by a plug-in could be included directly in your application without the plug-in. You could include the .jar files and write your code directly against the APIs. The point of plug-ins and the philosophy that most plug-in authors have embraced is that these external libraries should be as easy to work with as Grails itself. Plug-in authors tend to follow the principle of preferring convention to configuration but allowing configuration when it's desired. As we'll see shortly, the Searchable plug-in is an excellent example of this.

The Searchable plug-in allows us to perform full-text searches on all of the properties of our domain classes—even relationship properties. Let's take it for a spin. Install the plug-in at the command line while in our application's root directory:

```
$ grails install-plugin searchable
```

As the plug-in is fetched from the repository and installed, you will see a string of messages.

---

2. Developed by Maurice Nicholson; see http://grails.org/plugin/searchable.
3. The Twitter plug-in was developed by Burt Beckwith; for more, go to http://burtbeckwith.com.
4. http://www.winterwell.com/software/jtwitter.php

The final output looks something like this:

```
Thanks for installing the Grails Searchable Plugin!

Documentation is available at http://grails.org/Searchable+Plugin

Help is available from user@grails.codehaus.org

Issues and improvements should be raised at
    http://jira.codehaus.org/browse/GRAILSPLUGINS

If you are upgrading from a previous release,
    please see http://grails.org/Searchable+Plugin+-+Releases

Plugin searchable-0.5.4 installed
Plug-in provides the following new scripts:
----------------------------------------
grails install-searchable-config
```

Take particular notice of that last line. The install-searchable-config script
is what you use if the sensible defaults and conventional configuration
don't line up with what you need. This script will install a config file
that gives you much greater control over the features of the plug-in.

Now that the Searchable plug-in is installed, we are ready to start modifying our code to enable search. Let's start with TekDays/grails-app/domain/TekEvent.groovy. Open it, and add the highlighted code:

seek.1/TekDays/grails-app/domain/TekEvent.groovy

```
class TekEvent {
    String city
    String name
    TekUser organizer
    String venue
    Date startDate
    Date endDate
    String description

    String toString(){
        "$name, $city"
    }

►       static searchable = true

    static hasMany = [volunteers:TekUser,
                      respondents:String,
                      sponsorships:Sponsorship,
                      tasks:Task,
                      messages:Message]
```

```
static constraints = {
    name(blank:false)
    city(blank:false)
    description(maxSize : 5000)
    organizer(nullable:false)
    venue(nullable:true)
    startDate(nullable:true)
    endDate(nullable:true)
    volunteers(nullable : true)
    sponsorships(nullable : true)
    tasks(nullable : true)
    messages(nullable : true)
}
}
```

"What?!" you say—"Only one line?!" That was my initial reaction, too.
But it's true. That single line of code, static searchable = true, enables
full-text search of all the simple properties of the TekEvent. Let's put this
newfound power to use by adding a search action to our TekEventController. Open TekDays/grails-app/controllers/TekEventController.groovy, and
add the following action:

seek.1/TekDays/grails-app/controllers/TekEventController.groovy

```
def search = {
    if(params.query){
        def events = TekEvent.search(params.query).results
        [events : events]
    }
}
```

In this action, we start off with an **if** block to protect against a blank
search. Then we have two lines: the first calls the search() method that
the Searchable plug-in has added to the TekEvent class, passing in the
search query (which will come from a form we will be creating shortly).
The search() method returns a SearchResult instance, which contains a
results property that is a List. The next line just returns that list in a Map.
This action will, by convention, attempt to render a view in a file called
search.gsp, so let's give it one to render.

Create an empty file called TekDays/grails-app/views/tekEvent/search.gsp,
and add the following code:

seek.1/TekDays/grails-app/views/tekEvent/search.gsp

```
<html>
  <head>
    <meta http-equiv="Content-Type" content="text/html; charset=UTF-8"/>
    <meta name="layout" content="main" />
    <title>Tek Event Search Results</title>
  </head>
```

\\/ Joe Asks. . .
ᵔᶠ
ᵕ   **What If We Want to Search Associated Objects?**

At times, you may need to search for objects based on the properties of related objects. The Searchable plug-in makes this easy also. Let's say, for example, that you want to be able to search for TekEvent instances based on the properties of its organizer or volunteers. These are both of type TekUser, so add this line to the TekUser class:

static searchable = **true**

Now go to the TekEvent class, and change that searchable declaration to look like this:

```
static searchable = {
        organizer component: true
        volunteers component: true
}
```

All you did was turn TekUser into a *searchable* class. Then you used the Searchable plug-in's mapping DSL to tell it that the organizer and volunteers properties are *searchable components*. Notice that you don't have searchable = true anywhere in the TekEvent class; assigning a mapping closure to the searchable property automatically sets it to true.

There's a great deal more that can be done with the Searchable plug-in—much more than we can cover here. Fortunately, you can find extensive documentation at http://grails.org/plugin/searchable.

```
<body>
  <div class="nav">
    <span class="menuButton">
      <a class="home" href="${resource(dir:'')}">Home</a>
    </span>
  </div>
  <div class="body">
    <h1>Search Results</h1>
      <ul>
        <g:if test="${events}">
          <g:each in="${events}" var="event">
            <li>
              <g:link action="show" id="${event.id}">${event}</g:link>
            </li>
          </g:each>
```

```
          </g:if>
          <g:else>
            <h3>No Matching Results Found</h3>
          </g:else>
        </ul>
      </div>
    </div>
  </body>
</html>
```

The first part of this view is pretty much a copy of any of the other views we've created so far. After the "Search Results" heading, we create an unordered list. Next, we check to see whether we have any events. If we do, we use a *<g:each>* tag to iterate over the events and create a hyperlink list item for each one. If we don't have any events, we render an appropriate message.

At this point, we could actually run this code and begin searching, but we could do so only from the browser address bar with something like this: http:/localhost:8080/TekDays/tekEvent/search?query=perl. That's rather stone-age.

Instead, let's add a proper search field to our home page. Open TekDays/grails-app/views/index.gsp, and add the highlighted code right after the "Welcome" paragraph.

seek.1/TekDays/grails-app/views/index.gsp

```
        <h3>Welcome to TekDays.com</h3>
        <p>TekDays.com is a site dedicated to assisting individuals and communities
           to organize technology conferences.  To bring great minds with common
           interests and passions together for the good of greater geekdom!
        </p>
      </div>
►     <div id="homeSearch">
►       <g:form controller="tekEvent" action="search">
►         <label>Search:</label>
►         <input id="query" type="text" name="query" />
►         <input type=submit value="Go" />
►       </g:form>
►     </div>
```

We are using a *<g:form>* that will post to the search action of the tekEvent controller, and we have a single input element called query that will contain the search value. Finally, we have a submit element to fire it off. We're almost done.

Figure 10.3: TEKDAYS HOME PAGE WITH SEARCH

If we were to run this now, it would work, but we would be prompted to log in when we tried to perform a search. We want everyone to be able to find events on our site, so we'll have to fix this.

The security check is happening in our security filter, so we will modify it to allow the search action. Open TekDays/grails-app/conf/SecurityFilters. groovy, and add "search" to the allowedActions list, as shown on the next page.

seek.1/TekDays/grails-app/conf/SecurityFilters.groovy

```
class SecurityFilters {
  def filters = {
    doLogin(controller:'*', action:'*'){
      before = {
        def allowedActions = ['show', 'index', 'list', 'login',
                              'validate', 'search']
        if (!session.user && !allowedActions.contains(actionName)){
          redirect(controller:'tekUser', action:'login',
                params:['cName': controllerName, 'aName':actionName])
          return false
        }
      }
    }
  }
}
```

Great! Now when we load our home page, it looks like Figure 10.3, on the preceding page. Go ahead and try it. You can find events based on location, venue, name, and description. Our customer can find all the Groovy, Grails, and Griffon-related conferences that his heart desires. I'm sure he'll be happy.

10.4 Summary

In this iteration, we added some useful features for event organizers, volunteers, and users at large. Along the way, we learned about Criteria Builder for involved queries and about the Searchable plug-in for full-text search. We also got some more practice using those awesome Grails custom tags. The application is starting to look good and perform all kinds of handy functions. Our customer is anxious to put it to use and is already preparing some ideas for version 1.1.

In the next chapter, we'll add event registration and do some general refactoring based on feedback from our customer. We'll try more plug-ins and test some cool tricks with Grails URL mapping.

Chapter 11

Icing on the Cake

We are almost at the end of our project, and it is looking good. The customer is happy with our work, but he had a couple new feature requests. It happens. No worries, though. Because of the increased productivity of Grails and your own killer coding skills, we are ahead of schedule, so we should be able to fit these features in. Besides, that will give us the opportunity to try some more Grails plug-ins.

Let's take a look at what remains from our original feature list, and then we'll see whether we can fit in the extra goodies the customer asked for. This is all we have left from the first list:

- Customize event page
- Allow access to event home page with simple URL

Those shouldn't take too long. We should be able to get that done and also these new features:

- Make it easier for a user to volunteer for an event
- Provide a way for organizers to post news about event

Those sound like good ideas. With most other frameworks, this would be too much to take on in the time we have left, but with Grails, we can *code boldly*.

11.1 The Grails UI Plug-In

The first item on the new list is really just an improvement on one of the original features. We did provide a way for people to volunteer to help on events, but it's not very user friendly. So, we'll tackle this one right away. We'll add a button to the TekEvent show view that will allow logged-in users to volunteer to help on this event. When they click it, we'll show them a nice confirmation dialog box, and if they confirm, we'll add them to the volunteers collection for that event.

We'll start with the button. At first, that would seem as simple as adding a *<button>* tag somewhere on our page. But there is some logic involved. We don't want to show the button if the user is not logged in. Then if they are logged in, we don't want to show the button if they are already volunteering for this event. (I hope you can see where I'm heading with this.) We could do this with a couple of *<g:if>* tags, but our guilty consciences might drive us to depression. So instead, we will put this logic into a custom tag.

Open TekDays/grailsapp/taglib/TekDaysTagLib.groovy, and add the following tag closure:

```
icing/TekDays/grails-app/taglib/TekDaysTagLib.groovy
```

```groovy
def volunteerButton = {attrs ->
        if (session.user){
                def user = session.user.merge()
                def event = TekEvent.get(attrs.eventId)
                if (event && !event.volunteers.contains(user)){
                        out << "<span id='volunteerSpan' class='menuButton'>"
                    out << "<button id='volunteerButton' type='button'>"
                    out << "Volunteer For This Event"
                    out << "</button>"
                    out << "</span>"
        }
    }
}
```

If a user is logged in, there will be a TekUser in the session called user, so that's our first test. If we have a logged-in user, we'll use the eventId attribute to get the TekEvent instance. Then we grab the session.user and call the merge() method on it. (We need to do this because objects stored in the session become detached from the Hibernate session.) Once the user is merged, we can pass it to the contains() method of the event.volunteers to see whether this user is already a volunteer. If they are not, we'll go ahead and write out the button. We start with a *<span>* with a class of menuButton and id of volunteerSpan. Note this id; it will become important shortly.

Next we write out the *<button>* with its id and type, followed by the text of the button. We finish by closing up all our tags.

Figure 11.1: TEKEVENT SHOW VIEW MENU WITH VOLUNTEER BUTTON

Now we'll drop this tag in the navigation bar on the TekEvent show view, in TekDays/grails-app/views/tekEvent/show.gsp.

icing/TekDays/grails-app/views/tekEvent/show.gsp

```
<div class="nav">
  <span class="menuButton">
    <a class="home" href="${resource(dir:'')}">Home</a>
  </span>
  <span class="menuButton">
    <g:link class="list" action="list">TekEvent List</g:link>
  </span>
  <span class="menuButton">
    <g:link class="create" action="create">New TekEvent</g:link>
  </span>
  <span class="menuButton">
    <g:link class="list" controller="dashboard" action="dashboard"
            id="${tekEventInstance.id}">Event Dashboard</g:link>
  </span>
  <g:volunteerButton eventId="${tekEventInstance.id}" />
</div>
```

When a logged-in user views an event that they are not currently volunteering for, the menu bar will look like Figure 11.1. That looks good, but it doesn't do anything yet. Let's fix that next. What we want is a confirmation dialog box, followed by a call to an action that will add this user to the volunteers collection of this TekEvent. Since we don't want a boring JavaScript dialog box, we'll use the Grails UI plug-in to get a much more attractive one.

The Grails UI plug-in[1] wraps several Yahoo! User Interface[2] (YUI) components and thus makes it much easier to use them in a Grails

---

1. http://grails.org/plugin/grails-ui
2. You can find very detailed documentation on YUI at http://developer.yahoo.com/yui/.

application. Some of the components included are AutoComplete, Accordian, DataTable, and the one we're going to use, Dialog. The Grails UI plug-in, like Grails itself, brings ease of use to a complicated technology and still gives you deeper access when you need it. So, if you're familiar with the YUI component library, you won't have to trade power for simplicity.

Let's install the plug-in now. From the TekDays directory, run the following command:

```
$ grails install-plugin grails-ui
```

When the plug-in installs, it brings along everything it needs, so we are now ready to add the dialog box component to our TekEvent show view. You probably still have TekDays/grails-app/views/tekEvent/show.gsp open, so go ahead and add the highlighted line to the <head> section:

icing/TekDays/grails-app/views/tekEvent/show.gsp

```
  <head>
    <meta http-equiv="Content-Type" content="text/html; charset=UTF-8"/>
    <meta name="layout" content="main" />
▶   <gui:resources components="['dialog']"/>
    <title>Show TekEvent</title>
  </head>
```

The <gui:resources> tag is used to tell the plug-in which components we are using. It takes a list for its components attribute. If we were using more than one Grails UI component in this page, we would add them to the list.

Next, we need to add the <gui:dialog> tag that represents the Grails UI dialog component. Add the following code somewhere in the <body> section:

icing/TekDays/grails-app/views/tekEvent/show.gsp

```
<gui:dialog
     title="${'Volunteer for ' + tekEventInstance.name}"
     form="true"
     controller="tekEvent"
     action="volunteer"
     update="volunteerSpan"
     triggers="[show:[id:'volunteerButton', on:'click']]">
     <input type="hidden" name="id" value="${tekEventInstance.id}" />
   Welcome to the team!
   Your help will make a huge difference.
 </gui:dialog>
```

The *<gui:dialog>* tag takes several parameters and an optional body. We start with the title, for which we are using good old-fashioned String concatenation. I would prefer to do something like title="Volunteer for ${tekEventInstance.name}", but the component seems to ignore the space between the text and the expression. Good thing there are many ways to accomplish the same thing. Next, we set form to true. This will cause the dialog box to contain a form, which allows us to add form elements within the body as we'll discuss shortly. Since we have a form, we need to specify where the form should submit to. For this, we'll use the controller and action attributes. Now when the form/dialog box is submitted, it will call the TekEvent volunteer action.

Remember the ID that we added to the *<span>* tag in our taglib? We use that for the value of the update attribute. When we write the TekEvent volunteer, it will render some text that will replace the button in the volunteerSpan.

The last attribute that we are using is triggers. Triggers are elements that are used to call events on the dialog box. The most common, and the one we're using, is show. The triggers value is a Map with the key being the event name and the value being another Map. This nested Map contains the id of the element to be used and the event of that element that will call the trigger. You can also have the component create the trigger element for you like this: trigger="[show:[type:'button', text:'Volunteer For This Event', on:'click']]".

In the body of the tag, we have a hidden input that will hold the id of the current TekEvent. This will be passed by the form to the controller action so we can know which event the logged-in user is volunteering for. Then we have some text that will show up as the message of the dialog box. Finally, we close the *<gui:dialog>* tag.

OK. Our dialog box is all set up. We could even run this now and it would show up, but it would get a nasty error if we tried to submit. Let's create the volunteer action in TekDays/grails-app/controllers/TekEventController.groovy, like so:

icing/TekDays/grails-app/controllers/TekEventController.groovy

```
def volunteer = {
    def event = TekEvent.get(params.id)
    event.addToVolunteers(session.user)
    event.save()
    render "Thank you for Volunteering"
}
```

The volunteer action is the heart of this feature, even though it's only a few lines of code. First we use the id that was passed in the hidden input field to get the TekEvent instance. Then we add the logged-in user (session.user) to the volunteers collection. Next, we save the event, and finally, we render a text message. This text will replace the button in the volunteerSpan. This action is a great example of how the productivity of Grails doesn't come in scaffolding or code generation; it comes in the way you are able to accomplish so much with so little code. Scaffolding helps out as you start a new application, but this ability to enhance and expand your application quickly is where the real productivity gains come in.

We have one more thing to do before we see this in action. We need to tell the plug-in to use a YUI CSS class.[3] We'll do this in the *<body>* tag of TekDays/grails-app/views/layouts/main.gsp. Open this file, and modify the *<body>* tag, like so:

icing/TekDays/grails-app/views/layouts/main.gsp

```
<body class="yui-skin-sam">
```

Let's try it. Log someone in to the application, and navigate to an event that they haven't volunteered for. Click the button, and you should see something like Figure 11.2, on the next page. It's so easy that no one has an excuse for not volunteering.

11.2 The Twitter Plug-In

It seems that everyone is on Twitter[4] these days—even if they can't tell you why. We'll take advantage of this fact to help our hardworking event organizers get the word out about their events. If an event's organizer creates a Twitter account for their event, we will provide a form on the dashboard that will enable them to post updates to their event's Twitter timeline. To do this, we'll use the Twitter plug-in I mentioned earlier.

The Twitter plug-in gives us easy access to the JTwitter API.[5] We'll install it with the install-plugin script:

```
$ grails install-plugin twitter
```

---

3. There are rumors that this requirement will eventually be eliminated. Check the Grails plug-in portal (http://grails.org/plugins) for updates.
4. http://twitter.com
5. http://www.winterwell.com/software/jtwitter.php

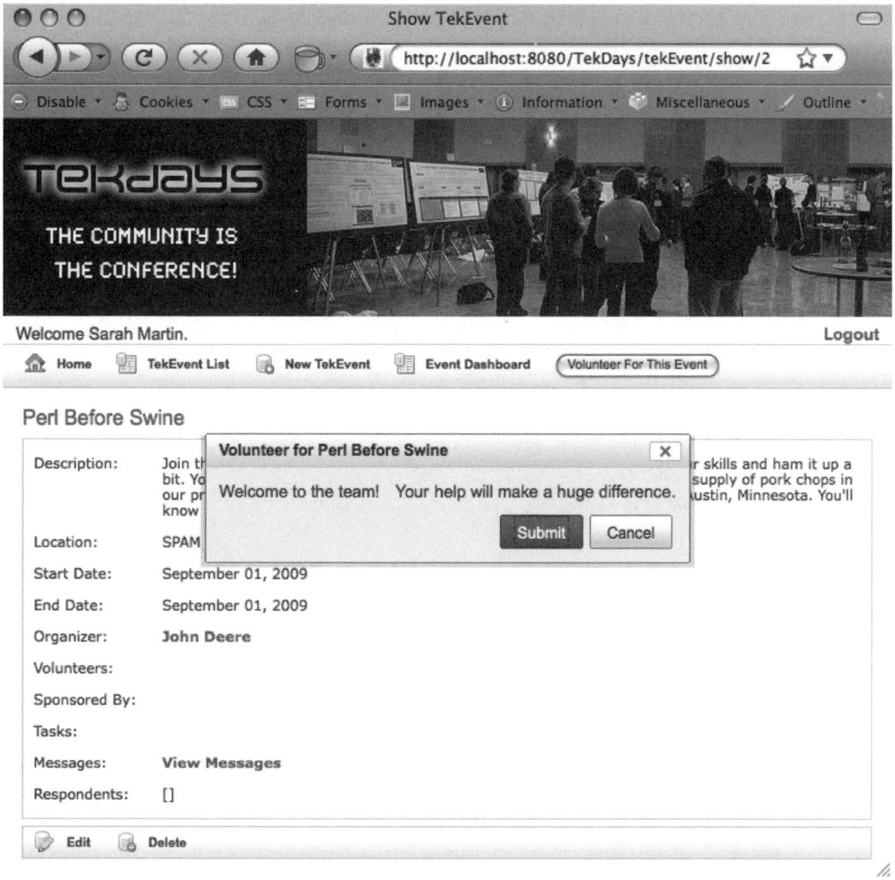

Figure 11.2: THE VOLUNTEER DIALOG BOX

This plug-in provides a service class (TwitterService) with a host of methods that interact with Twitter. We'll be using only a couple of these methods, but you can read about the rest of them in the excellent documentation at http://grails.org/plugin/twitter.

Before we get started with the plug-in, we need to modify the TekEvent to hold the information that allows the organizer to log in to the event's Twitter account.

Open TekDays/grails-app/domain/TekEvent.groovy, and add the highlighted lines:

icing/TekDays/grails-app/domain/TekEvent.groovy

```
class TekEvent {
    String city
    String name
    TekUser organizer
    String venue
    Date startDate
    Date endDate
    String description
▶   String twitterId
▶   String twitterPassword

    String toString(){
        "$name, $city"
    }

        static searchable = true

    static hasMany = [volunteers:TekUser,
                      respondents:String,
                      sponsorships:Sponsorship,
                      tasks:Task,
                      messages:Message]

    static constraints = {
        name(blank:false)
        city(blank:false)
        description(maxSize : 5000)
        organizer(nullable:false)
        venue(nullable:true)
        startDate(nullable:true)
        endDate(nullable:true)
        volunteers(nullable : true)
        sponsorships(nullable : true)
        tasks(nullable : true)
        messages(nullable : true)
▶       twitterId(nullable:true)
▶       twitterPassword(nullable:true)
    }
}
```

We gave the twitterId and twitterPassword the constraint nullable:true, since this is an optional feature.

Now we need to provide a way to enter these new properties. We'll add two input fields to the create view.

Open TekDays/grails-app/views/tekEvent/create.gsp, and add <tr> blocks
for twitterId and twitterPassword, like so:

icing/TekDays/grails-app/views/tekEvent/create.gsp

```
<tr class="prop">
  <td valign="top" class="name">
    <label for="twitterId">TwitterId / Nickname:</label>
  </td>
  <td valign="top">
    <input type="text"
           id="twitterId"
           name="twitterId"
           value="${fieldValue(bean:tekEventInstance,field:'twitterId')}"/>
  </td>
</tr>
<tr class="prop">
  <td valign="top" class="name">
    <label for="twitterPassword">Twitter Password:</label>
  </td>
  <td valign="top">
    <input type="password"
           id="twitterPassword"
           name="twitterPassword"
           value="${fieldValue(bean:tekEventInstance,field:'twitterPassword')}"/>
  </td>
</tr>
```

We added two input fields, with corresponding labels. Note that we set
the label of the twitterId to "TwitterId / Nickname." We'll be using this
property for another purpose shortly. We don't have to do anything to
the controller for these new properties to be saved; GORM will take care
of that. We do need to add the same fields to the edit view, but we won't
take space to show that, since it's exactly the same code.

Now we can start putting the TwitterService to use. We'll add a new action
to the DashboardController, because we're going to expose this feature in
the organizer's dashboard. Open TekDays/grails-app/controllers/Dashboard-
Controller.groovy, and add the following code:

icing/TekDays/grails-app/controllers/DashboardController.groovy

```
class DashboardController {

    def twitterService
    //Existing dashboard code snipped
    def tweet = {
            def event = TekEvent.get(params.id)
            if (event){
                    twitterService.setStatus(params.status,
```

```
                                        [username:event.twitterId,
                                         password:event.twitterPassword])
            }
            redirect(action:dashboard, id:event.id)
        }
}
```

Note that we are defining a property called twitterService at the top of the class. When we declare that property using the convention of changing the first character of the class name to lowercase, Grails will inject a TwitterService instance into our controller at runtime. Next we add our tweet action, which starts out by getting the current TekEvent. If we have a valid instance, we call the setStatus() method of the TwitterService. This method takes the status to post and a map containing the Twitter credentials. That's all there is to it! Most of the other methods of the TwitterService are just as simple, and perhaps for version 1.1 we can add more Twitter integration since it's so easy to do. But for now, this gives us just what we need. Finally, we redirect to the dashboard so they can do it all over again.

Now we'll add a new section to the dashboard to call this action. Open TekDays/grails-app/views/dashboard/dashboard.gsp, and add the highlighted code:

icing/TekDays/grails-app/views/dashboard/dashboard.gsp

```
        <div id="sponsors" style='margin:10px 10px 10px 10px'>
          <g:render template="sponsors" model="${[sponsorships:sponsorships]}" />
        </div>
▶       <g:if test="${event.twitterId}">
▶         <div id="twitter" style='margin:10px 10px 10px 10px'>
▶           <g:render template="twitter" model="${[event:event]}" />
▶         </div>
▶       </g:if>
      </body>
</html>
```

We're going to put the specifics of our Twitter feature in a template. In the dashboard view, we'll render this template if the TekEvent instance has a value assigned to its twitterId property. (We're using a <g:if> tag for this since it's only a single test, but I must admit my custom tag trigger finger is twitching.)

Forum Messages

Author	Subject	Content
John Doe	Can anyone recommend a good screen printer?	I need to get a quote on ...
Sarah Martin	I think I can get James Gosling to do a keynote	I know a guy who knows a ...
John Doe	Welcome to the Gateway Code Camp Forum	Welcome to the Gateway Co ...

View threaded messages for this event.

Sponsors

Name	Web Site	Contribution
Object Computing Incorporated	ociweb.com	Venue
Contegix	contegix.com	Other

Post Event Updates to gatewaycode's Twitter Timeline
(No more than 140 characters)

Post to Twitter

Figure 11.3: SECTION OF DASHBOARD VIEW WITH TWITTER FORM

Now we'll create the template. Create a blank file called TekDays/grails-app/views/dashboard/_twitter.gsp, and add the following code:

`icing/TekDays/grails-app/views/dashboard/_twitter.gsp`

```
<h3>Post Event Updates to ${event.twitterId}'s Twitter Timeline</h3>
<g:form name="twitterForm" action="tweet" id="${event.id}">
(No more than 140 characters)<br/>
<textarea name="status" rows="3" columns="50" style="width:100%;height:60">
</textarea><br/>
<input type="submit" value="Post to Twitter" />
</g:form>
```

We start off our Twitter template with a heading in which we include the event's twitterId, using a Groovy expression. Then we use <g:form> to create a form that will post to the tweet action and pass the event.id. We have only one input in our form: a <textarea> called status. This will contain the status message to post to Twitter. We finish with a standard submit button. Now we're ready to tweet!

In Figure 11.3, we can see the bottom half of the dashboard view, which includes our new Twitter section. To test this, you can enter your own Twitter credentials and post a message starting with @daveklein. I'll let you know if it worked.

11.3 Making the Event Page Customizable with the Blurb Plug-In

We need to make the TekEvent show view more customizable. Organizers can already change the name and description, but we're going to add the ability to have a section of the page that they can choose to use, and change easily, or to not use. And since this extra content field will be optional, we won't clutter up our domain model with it. Instead, we'll use the simple but handy Blurb plug-in.[6]

The Blurb plug-in provides a domain class called Blurb, which has name and content properties. It also provides a GSP tag to show the content of a Blurb by its name property. To get started, we'll install the plug-in in the usual way:

```
$ grails install-plugin blurb
```

The plug-in also includes a controller and views to work with blurbs, but we're not going to use those. We'll just treat the Blurb as if it were a domain class in our application. We'll change the dashboard view and the DashboardController to allow organizers to view and edit their blurbs, and we'll add the <g:blurb> tag to our show view.

Let's start with the controller. Open TekDays/grails-app/controllers/DashboardController.groovy, and add the highlighted lines to the following block of code:

```
icing/TekDays/grails-app/controllers/DashboardController.groovy
        if (event){
            if(event.organizer.userName == session.user.userName ||
               event.volunteers.collect{it.userName}.contains(
                                              session.user.userName)){
                def tasks = Task.findAllByEventAndCompleted(event, false,
                                                [max:5, sort:'dueDate']
                def volunteers = event.volunteers
                def messages = Message.findAllByEventAndParentIsNull(event,
                                                            [sort:'id',
                                                            order:'desc']
                def sponsorships = event.sponsorships
  ▶             def blurb = Blurb.findByName("custom_${event.id}")
  ▶             if (!blurb){
  ▶                 blurb = new Blurb(name:"custom_${event.id}",
  ▶                                 content:"").save()
  ▶             }
                return [event:event, tasks:tasks, volunteers:volunteers,
                        messages:messages, sponsorships:sponsorships,
  ▶                     blurb:blurb]
            }
```

---

6. http://grails.org/plugin/blurb

```
    else{
      flash.message = "Access to dashboard for ${event.name} denied."
      redirect(controller:'tekEvent', action:'list')
    }
  }
}
```

We first define a variable called blurb and try to retrieve the Blurb for this event, using a convention that includes the event.id. If we don't find one, we create and save one. Note that there is no relationship between the TekEvent and the Blurb, so we do need to save the Blurb explicitly. Then we add the blurb to the returned Map. This will make it available to the dashboard view. We will also need a way to save changes to the Blurb, so let's add a new action to the controller:

icing/TekDays/grails-app/controllers/DashboardController.groovy

```
def updateBlurb = {
        def blurb = Blurb.get(params.id)
        blurb.content = params.content
        blurb.save()
        redirect(action:'dashboard', id:params.eventId)
}
```

Here we are retrieving a Blurb instance based on the id parameter passed in from a form that we will be creating in the dashboard view. We then assign its content to the content found in the params and save it. Finally, we redirect back to the dashboard view.

Now let's turn our attention to the dashboard view. Open TekDays/grails-app/views/dashboard/dashboard.gsp, and add the highlighted section:

icing/TekDays/grails-app/views/dashboard/dashboard.gsp

```
    <div id="event" style='margin:10px 10px 10px 10px'>
      <g:render template="event" model="${[event:event]}" />
    </div>
►   <div id="blurb" style='margin:10px 10px 10px 10px'>
►     <g:render template="blurb" model="${[blurb:blurb, event:event]}" />
►   </div>
    <div id="tasks" style='margin:10px 10px 10px 10px'>
      <g:render template="tasks" model="${['tasks':tasks]}" />
    </div>
```

In keeping with our earlier design decision to separate the different features of the dashboard view into templates, all we will add to this page is another <div> tag wrapping a <g:render> tag, which will render the _blurb.gsp template, passing the blurb in the model.

Next we need to create the template. The template will contain a form with a <textarea> in which event organizers can enter their custom

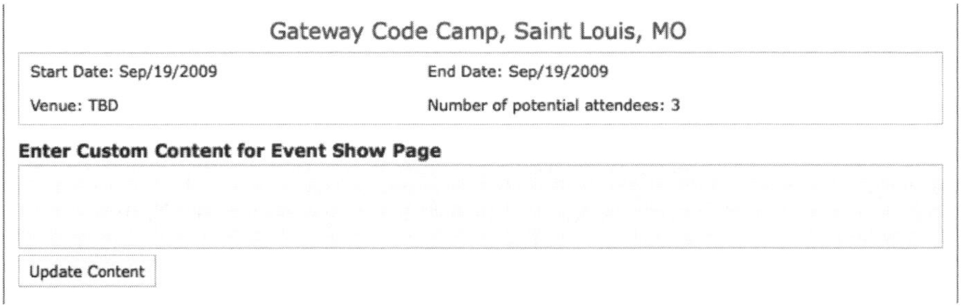

Gateway Code Camp, Saint Louis, MO

Start Date: Sep/19/2009	End Date: Sep/19/2009
Venue: TBD	Number of potential attendees: 3

Enter Custom Content for Event Show Page

Update Content

Figure 11.4: SECTION OF DASHBOARD VIEW WITH BLURB FORM

content. Create a new file called TekDays/grails-app/views/dashboard/ _blurb.gsp, and add the following code:

```
icing/TekDays/grails-app/views/dashboard/_blurb.gsp
<h3>Enter Custom Content for Event Show Page</h3>
<g:form name="blurbForm" action="updateBlurb" id="${blurb?.id}">
  <textarea name="content" cols="60" rows="3"
            style="width:100%; height:60px">${blurb?.content}</textarea>
  <br/>
  <input type="hidden" name="eventId" value="${event?.id}">
  <input type="submit" value="Update Content">
</g:form>
```

Here we have a simple heading, which is a *<g:form>* tag that will submit to the updateBlurb action, a *<textarea>*, and a submit button. If we look at the dashboard view, now we can see the new custom blurb form, shown in Figure 11.4.

At this point, we can view and edit the custom content, but we aren't using it anywhere. Let's add the *<g:blurb>* tag to the TekEvent show view and clean up the view a bit while we're there. Open TekDays/grails-app/views/tekEvent/show.gsp, and let's take a look at what we have there. (You can also refer to Figure 9.4, on page 156.) We can see that we are displaying information about the event that potential attendees, or even potential volunteers, don't really need to see. Much of this information is already available in the dashboard view. So, let's clean some of that out. We can see that each property is contained in a *<tr>* block. This makes it easy to cleanly remove or rearrange properties as we need.

```
<div class="body">
  <h1>${fieldValue(bean:tekEventInstance, field:'name')}</h1>
  <g:if test="${flash.message}">
    <div class="message">${flash.message}</div>
  </g:if>
  <div class="dialog">
    <table>
      <tbody>
        <tr class="prop">
          <td valign="top" class="name">Description:</td>
          <td valign="top" class="value">
            ${fieldValue(bean:tekEventInstance, field:'description')}
          </td>
        </tr>
        <tr class="prop">
          <td valign="top" class="name">Location:</td>
          <td valign="top" class="value">
            ${fieldValue(bean:tekEventInstance, field:'venue')},
              ${fieldValue(bean:tekEventInstance, field:'city')}
          </td>
        </tr>
        </tr>
        <tr class="prop">
          <td valign="top" class="name">Start Date:</td>
          <td valign="top" class="value">
            <g:formatDate format="MMMM dd, yyyy"
                      date="${tekEventInstance.startDate}"/>
          </td>
        </tr>
        </tr>
        <tr class="prop">
          <td valign="top" class="name">End Date:</td>
          <td valign="top" class="value">
            <g:formatDate format="MMMM dd, yyyy"
                      date="${tekEventInstance.endDate}"/>
          </td>
        </tr>
        <tr class="prop">
          <td valign="top" class="name">Sponsored By:</td>
          <td  valign="top" style="text-align:left;" class="value">
            <ul>
              <g:each var="s" in="${tekEventInstance.sponsorships}">
                <li><g:link controller="sponsorship" action="show" id="${s.id}">
                  ${s.sponsor?.encodeAsHTML()}
                </g:link></li>
              </g:each>
            </ul>
          </td>
        </tr>
      </tbody>
```

```
                         </table>
    ▶                    <div style="width:100%">
    ▶                      <g:blurb name="custom_${tekEventInstance?.id}" />
    ▶                    </div>
                       </div>
                       <div class="buttons">
                         <g:form>
                           <input type="hidden" name="id" value="${tekEventInstance?.id}" />
                           <span class="button">
                             <g:actionSubmit class="edit" value="Edit" />
                           </span>
                           <span class="button">
                             <g:actionSubmit class="delete"
                                 onclick="return confirm('Are you sure?');" value="Delete" />
                           </span>
                         </g:form>
                       </div>
                     </div>
                   </body>
```

The organizer, volunteers, tasks, and messages are already covered in the
dashboard, so let's get rid of them. Then, just below the *<table>*, we
added the *<g:blurb>* tag with the name that is created based on our
convention. If the event doesn't have a Blurb instance or if it has one
that is blank, nothing will render.

Go ahead and give one of our events some custom content, and see how
it looks. You can get an idea from Figure 11.5, on the next page.

11.4 User-Friendly URLs

Now that we have this nicer-looking and customizable event page, we
need to provide a way to access it using a simple URL. The way it stands
now, once the application is deployed, the URL to a specific event's
page looks something like this: http://TekDays.com/tekEvent/show/5024753.
(OK, the id might not be quite that large at first, but we're thinking
positive here.) Our customer would like us to get to something more
like http://TekDays.com/events/MyTekEvent. This will make it easier for the
event organizers and volunteers to plaster links all over the Internet for
their event.

As we have come to expect, Grails provides a simple way to do this.
Every Grails application has a UrlMappings class, which uses a DSL[7] to
build URL mappings. The conventional Grails mappings are in there by

---

7. Domain-specific language.

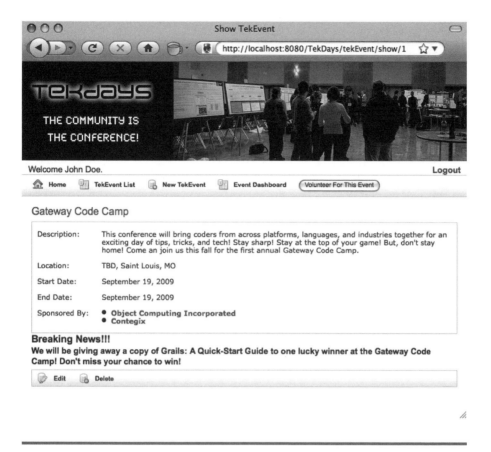

Figure 11.5: CUSTOMIZABLE EVENT SHOW VIEW

default, and we can add as many different mappings as needed. Let's take a look at the default mappings to get an idea of how this works. Open TekDays/grails-app/conf/UrlMappings.groovy:

```groovy
class UrlMappings {
    static mappings = {
      "/$controller/$action?/$id?"{
          constraints {
                      // apply constraints here
              }
        }
      "/"(view:"/index")
      "500"(view:'/error')
    }
}
```

The static mappings block is the heart of the UrlMappings class. Inside this block we see the mappings for the conventional Grails behavior. The first value found after the root (/) will be assigned to the controller variable. The next value will be assigned to the action, and the last one will be assigned to the id. The first variable, controller, is required; the other two have a ? on the end, which marks them as optional. What this means is that any URL with one, two, or three values after the root will match this mapping and be applied accordingly. For example, /foo would be mapped to the FooController's default action, /foo/bar would be mapped to the bar action of FooController, and /foo/bar/baz would be mapped to the bar action of FooController with an id parameter of baz. You get the picture.

Inside the mapping block there is an empty constraints block, where we can put constraints on the different variables, much as we did earlier on domain class properties. After this, we have the two other default mappings. The root mapping, when nothing but the application root is in the URL, maps directly to the index view. Mapping directly to a view makes sense for pages that don't need any data; for example, you might use this for an About page. Last of all, we have the 500 error mapping.

Let's add another mapping that will match the URLs that we want to support. The code should look something like this:

icing/TekDays/grails-app/conf/UrlMappings.groovy

```
"/events/$nickname"{
    controller = "tekEvent"
    action = "show"
}
```

The default Grails mapping uses all variables. Our mapping is using a static value (events) and a variable ($nickname). Since our mapping does not include variables for controller and action, we need to set those inside the mapping block. This mapping will match any URL that starts with the word events and has one more value, which will be assigned to the variable $nickname. The matched URL will be directed to the show action of TekEventController with a nickname parameter. So, now we need to make use of the nickname.

We're going to modify the show action to use a nickname parameter to show a TekEvent instance. Before we do that, though, we need to determine what we are going to use for the nickname. Remember the twitterId that we added for the Twitter plug-in? We labeled the input field for that property "TwitterId / Nickname" because we're going to use it for *that* purpose too. It's quite a good fit, since a Twitter ID is usually something short and easy to remember. Let's get to work.

Open TekDays/grails-app/controllers/TekEventController.groovy, and modify the show action as shown here:

```
icing/TekDays/grails-app/controllers/TekEventController.groovy

def show = {
        def tekEventInstance
        if (params.nickname){
                tekEventInstance = TekEvent.findByTwitterId(params.nickname)
        }
        else
     tekEventInstance = TekEvent.get( params.id )

    if(!tekEventInstance) {
            if (params.nickname)
            flash.message = "TekEvent not found with id ${params.id}"
        else
            flash.message = "TekEvent not found with nickname ${params.nickname}"
        redirect(action:list)
    }
    else { return [ tekEventInstance : tekEventInstance ] }
}
```

This action's job is to retrieve a TekEvent instance and pass it to the show view. All we're doing here is giving it another way of retrieving the TekEvent. To do this, we first separate the variable *declaration* from the *assignment*. Then we use an **if** to decide whether to retrieve the instance by nickname or by id. If there's a nickname value in the params, we use the dynamic finder findByTwitterId(). Then, to make our error messages clearer in case we don't find an instance, we use another **if** block to determine the appropriate error message to display.

I added the twitterId of "GatewayCode" to one of our test events, so now we can navigate to http://localhost:8080/TekDays/events/GatewayCode and get something like Figure 11.6, on the following page.

11.5 Summary

We did it! We completed the original feature list for TekDays and even added a couple of bonus features with the time we saved by using Grails. We also saw firsthand how powerful and easy to use Grails plug-ins are. (Be sure to browse the Grails plug-in portal at http://grails.org/plugin/home to see what others are available.)

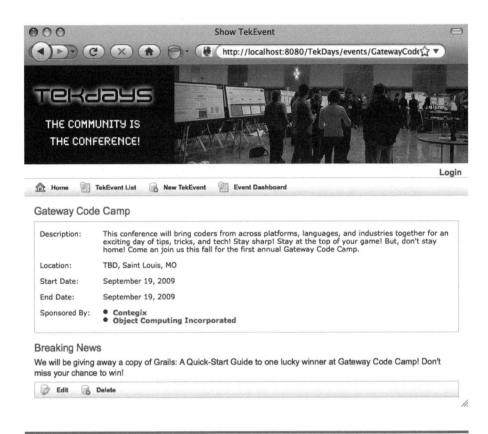

Figure 11.6: CUSTOMIZABLE EVENT SHOW VIEW

All that's left to do now is to deploy the application to our server. Before you start thinking "Ant and Ivy and Maven, oh my!" remember that this is *Grails* we're talking about. Well, you'll see. Turn the page.

Deployment and Beyond

We are nearing the end of our project and our time together. We've accomplished quite a bit, and our customer is happy with the results. He's also very impressed with how quickly we got it done. He's just about ready for us to hand the application over to him, but he wants us to try deploying it first—sort of as a sanity check.

Up until now, we've been running TekDays in Jetty,[1] which is an HTTP server and Java servlet container. Some people also use Jetty for production deployment, but usually production will use something a little more heavy-duty, such as Tomcat,[2] or a full-blown JEE[3] server, such as WebLogic, JBoss, or, if they can't find a way out of it, WebSphere.

Grails applications will run well on any of these. For our purposes (and for most Grails applications), Tomcat will be a good fit. If you don't have Tomcat and would like to follow along, you can download it at http://tomcat.apache.org/download-60.cgi, or you can use any other standards-compliant Java servlet container.

12.1 Using a JNDI Data Source

Before packaging our application for deployment, we need to change our data source. Open TekDays/grails-app/conf/DataSource.groovy.

---

1. http://www.mortbay.org/jetty
2. http://tomcat.apache.org
3. Java Enterprise Edition

When we last worked on this file, it looked something like this:

```
dataSource {
  pooled = true
  driverClassName = "com.mysql.jdbc.Driver"
  username = "dave"
  password = "1234"
}
hibernate {
    cache.use_second_level_cache=true
    cache.use_query_cache=true
    cache.provider_class='com.opensymphony.oscache.hibernate.OSCacheProvider'
}
// environment specific settings
environments {
  development {
        dataSource {
          dbCreate = "update"//one of 'create', 'create-drop','update'
          url = "jdbc:mysql://localhost:3306/tekdays"
        }
  }
  test {
        dataSource {
                dbCreate = "update"
                url = "jdbc:hsqldb:mem:testDb"
        }
  }
  production {
        dataSource {
                dbCreate = "update"
                url = "jdbc:hsqldb:file:prodDb;shutdown=true"
        }
  }
}
```

Our focus now is on the production block toward the end of the file. It currently points to an in-memory HSQLDB database. It may seem obvious, but there *have* been incidents where applications went into production this way. It's not a good thing. So, we're going to make sure we get this changed.

Now, we could change the production dataSource to point to a MySQL instance, as we did for the development dataSource, but in most organizations it's considered bad form to include database credentials in an application configuration file. All JEE servers and virtually all Java servlet containers support the Java Naming and Directory Interface (JNDI).[4] And at the risk of once again sounding like a broken record, Grails makes it incredibly easy to use a JNDI data source.

---

4. http://java.sun.com/products/jndi/

> ### ⚬ Joe Asks…
> #### JEE Server, Java Servlet Container: What's the Difference?
>
> *JEE server* and *Java servlet container* are often used almost as interchangeable terms. They aren't the same thing, but they are related. A *JEE server* is an application server that implements the JEE specification. This specification includes things like EJB, JMS, JPA, JTA, JSP, Servlets, JSF, and more. (Don't worry if you don't recognize all of these.)
>
> A *Java servlet container* usually supports a subset of those JEE components, such as JSP, Servlets, and JSF—basically the web-related JEE components. Some servlet containers are gradually taking on more components, so these lines are beginning to blur.
>
> A simple way to look at it is that a servlet container is a lightweight JEE server.

Our customer studied up on the subject at http://tomcat.apache.org/tomcat-6.0-doc/jndi-resources-howto.html and has configured a JNDI data source in his Tomcat server named TekDaysDS. To direct our application to use that data source, we'll change the production block of Data-Source.groovy like this:

`deploy/TekDays/grails-app/conf/DataSource.groovy`

```
production {
        dataSource {
                jndiName = "java:comp/env/jdbc/TekDaysDS"
        }
}
```

That's all there is to it. The exact layout of the JNDI string may vary with different servers, so if you're working with something other than Tomcat, refer to your server's documentation for more details. The production database URL and credentials will now be read from the server. The default values will still be used for development and test environments.

12.2 Creating and Deploying a WAR

The standard way to deploy a Java-based web application is as a web application resource (WAR) file. There are many tools available to help package a web application into a WAR, from IDEs such as Eclipse and NetBeans to build tools such as Ant and Maven. With Grails, however, those things are rarely needed. A simple Grails script will do it for us.

```
$ grails war
```

That single script will compile our source code, pull in our dependencies, and bundle it all into a standard JEE WAR file. For our project, the default name for this file is TekDays-0.1.war. Deploying this to Tomcat is as simple as copying the file to Tomcat's webapps directory and restarting.

Our app deploys successfully on Tomcat. We're good to go...for now. No software application is ever really done; TekDays may be ready to start using, but it can always be improved.

12.3 Next Steps

I'm sure that as we've worked on this project, you've thought of features that would be nice to have in TekDays, or perhaps different ways to implement features. Go for it! With the rapid feedback and flexible, dynamic nature of Grails, it's easy to explore and experiment.

You could look through the list of Grails plug-ins at http://grails.org/plugin/home and see which ones might be useful—and perhaps add a regional event calendar, or use the Grails mail plug-in[5] to add email services to the application. Or you may have noticed that we don't yet have any facility for speakers or sessions. (Our customer was mostly interested in organizing open spaces conferences.)

But before you get too carried away with changes to this production system, there are a couple of things to consider: version control and database migration.

As I said earlier, Grails makes experimentation fun and easy, but you don't want to experiment with production code. You also don't want to start making duplicate project directories all over the place. So first of all, move the project into a version control system such as SVN or Git. You can find information about using SVN with Grails at http://www.grails.org/Checking+Projects+into+SVN. Git is a distributed version control system that is becoming quite popular. (In fact, the Grails source code

---

5. http://grails.org/plugin/mail

has been moved into Git.) There's a great screencast with Jeff Brown showing how to use Git with Grails at http://grails.org/Grails+Screencasts.

A database migration tool can help prevent database nightmares as you begin making changes to the database to implement new features. The Autobase plug-in[6] by Robert Fischer integrates the Liquibase framework with Grails, helping you avoid those nightmares and rest easy as you migrate your database from version to version.

Feel free to take our application in different directions or to just borrow ideas from it and start something new. If you want to see where I'm taking this idea, check out http://TekDays.com or http://gquick.blogspot.com.

12.4 Parting Thoughts

Now, feeling a bit like Mr. Rogers at the end of the show (am I dating myself here?), it's time for me to take off my customer hat, my project manager hat, and my development team member hat and to put on my author hat. The goal of this book was to give you, the reader, a hands-on tutorial of web development with Grails: to demonstrate enough features and provide enough practice to get you past the newbie stage and on your way to mastery. It's my hope that you've learned enough to be productive with Grails. Even more, I hope that you caught a vision of the power, productivity, and pleasure of Grails.

Because this was a quick-start guide and not an in-depth reference, there are areas that I only touched on and where more information would be helpful. To that end, I've included an appendix that lists books, articles, websites, and blogs that will help you dig deeper. In the appendix, I'll also introduce you to the G3 community.[7] The community is truly one of the biggest strengths of these technologies.

Finally, I hope you learned as much and had as much fun working through this book as I had writing it.

---

6. http://grails.org/plugin/autobase

7. G3 stands for Groovy, Grails, and Griffon. Griffon (http://griffon.codehaus.org) is an MVC framework for rich desktop development with Groovy.

Additional CSS Rules

Here are some style rules that we have added to TekDays/web-app/css/main.css. Please copy these to your project to make it easier to follow along with the project in the book.

```css
/*Dashboard*/
.dashItem {
    margin: 10px;
}
#eventBlurb {
    width: 100%;
    height: 60px;
}
#dashHeader {
    text-align: center;
}

/*Index*/
#homeSearch {
    margin-left: 30%;
    margin-top: 25px;
    width: 40%;
}
#homeSearch label {
    font-weight: bold;
}
#welcome {
    margin-left: 25px;
    margin-top: 25px;
    width: 85%;
}
.homeCell {
    margin-left: 25px;
    margin-top: 25px;
    width: 85%;
}
```

```
.homeCell .buttons {
    float: right;
    margin-right: 30px;
}

/*Message Create*/
.messageField {
    width:550px
}

/*Ajaxlist*/
#messageList {
    overflow:auto
}
```

Appendix B

Resources

Now that you're up and running with Grails, you'll want to learn more, and you will undoubtedly have questions. What follows is a Grails resource guide, and then some. Since Grails is part of the greater Groovy community (what I refer to as the G3 Community),[1] this guide will point you to resources beyond Grails alone. These are the resources that I've used and/or that are made available by people who I know and respect; I trust that you'll find them useful as well.

B.1   Online Resources

The Internet has more than you'll ever need to know about most things, Groovy and Grails included. The following is a (very abbreviated) list of general websites and mailing lists that are worth checking out.

Grails: A Quick-Start Guide Blog .... http://gquick.blogspot.com
Additional tips, tricks and tutorials that build on the example from the book.

Official Grails website . . . . .http://grails.org

Official Groovy website . . . . http://groovy.codehaus.org

Official Griffon website . . . . .http://griffon.codehaus.org

The Grails plug-in portal . . . . http://grails.org/plugin/home
A gold mine of plug-in information. Besides a complete list of the plug-ins,

---

1. G3 stands for Groovy, Grails, and Griffon.

there's documentation, tutorials, screencasts, and more. Comments and a rating system help you determine whether a plug-in is right for you and help you choose between competing plug-ins.

Grails mailing lists . . . . http://grails.org/Mailing+lists
The Grails user and dev lists are quite active and loaded with helpful people. Don't be afraid to ask for help, and as you get more comfortable with the framework, don't be afraid to offer help. It's a great feeling when you go from just asking questions to answering them too.

Groovy mailing lists . . . . http://groovy.codehaus.org/Mailing+Lists
Sometimes your question will be more Groovy language-specific. When this happens, the folks on this list are quick to help. Also, if you are new to Groovy, taking some time to read through the threads on this list is a great way to learn more about the language.

GroovyBlogs. . . . . .http://groovyblogs.org
This is an excellent blog aggregator currently covering more than 250 blogs related to Groovy technologies.

Grails Tutorials . . . . http://grailstutorials.com/home
Loaded with tips, tricks, examples, and of course tutorials, this is another site to bookmark and check often.

GrailsCrowd. . . . . .http://grailscrowd.com
GrailsCrowd is a social networking site for Groovy and Grails developers. You can connect with hundreds of other developers around the world. You can see who's doing what in your area and let the world know about projects you're working on.

GroovyTweets. . . . . .http://groovytweets.org
Groovy Tweets is a Twitter aggregator and ranking engine. It's also a great way to find all the Groovy folks on Twitter. Just go to http://twitter.com/groovytweets and check out the *following* list.

B.2   Meet the G3 Community

I've heard many people say this, and I wholeheartedly agree: one of the best things about Groovy, Grails, and Griffon is the community. The developers involved in these technologies are some of the smartest, most enthusiastic, and most helpful people I've worked with. I've had the pleasure of meeting many of them in person at various conferences; others I know only through the ether. But I consider it an honor to work with and be associated with them. Here's an introduction to some of your new colleagues.

The Grails Dev Team

Graeme Rocher . . . . http://graemerocher.blogspot.com
Graeme is the Grails project lead and a coauthor of *The Definitive Guide to Grails*.

Marc Palmer . . . . http://www.anyware.co.uk
Marc is a Grails committer and author of several Grails plug-ins.

Dierk König http://www.amazon.com/gp/blog/A368TUB0Q1IE3F
Dierk is a Grails committer and the lead author of *Groovy in Action*.

Jason Rudolph . . . . http://jasonrudolph.com
Jason is a Grails committer and author of *Getting Started with Grails*.

Jeff Brown . . . . http://javajeff.blogspot.com
Jeff is a Grails committer and coauthor of *The Definitive Guide to Grails*.

Marcel Overdijk . . . . http://marceloverdijk.blogspot.com
Marcel is a Grails committer and author of several Grails plug-ins.

Sergey Nebolsin . . . . http://snebolsin.blogspot.com
Sergey's a Grails committer and the author of the Quartz plug-in, among others.

Lee Butts . . . . http://www.leebutts.com
Lee is a Grails committer, plug-in contributor, and car buff.

The Grails Podcast Team

Sven and Glen are the hosts of the Grails Podcast. For details, see Section B.3, *Other Media*, on page 209.

Sven Haiges . . . . http://hansamann.wordpress.com
Sven is the founder of the Grails Podcast and the creator of GroovyTweets.org.

Glen Smith . . . . http://blogs.bytecode.com.au/glen
Glen is the creator of GroovyBlogs.org and coauthor of *Grails in Action*.

Other G3 Bloggers

There are currently over 250 blogs aggregated on GroovyBlogs.org. I'm not going to list them all here, but these are some members of the community who have made (and are making) significant contributions. Their blogs are a rich source of information and experience, as well as a way to get to know them. When you come across them later on the mailing list or bump into them at a conference, it'll be like seeing an old friend.

Andres Almiray . . . . http://www.jroller.com/aalmiray
Andres is a Groovy committer, a member of the core Griffon development team, a Grails plug-in developer, and coauthor of the upcoming *Griffon in Action*.

Burt Beckwith: An Army of Solipsists . . . . http://burtbeckwith.com/blog
Burt is a prolific plug-in author and a regular on the Grails mailing lists. Burt also served as the technical editor for the book *Grails in Action*.

Luke Daley . . . . http://www.ldaley.com
Luke is a Grails plug-in author and the creator of the TextMate Groovy/Grails bundle and of the GLDAPO (Groovy LDAP) library.

Hamlet D'Arcy: Behind the Times . . . . http://hamletdarcy.blogspot.com
Hamlet is a Groovy committer and AST wizard.

Scott Davis: Musings on Java and Open Source . . .
. . . http://davisworld.org/blojsom/blog/
Scott is a Groovy and Grails trainer, frequent conference speaker, and author of several books, including *Groovy Recipes: Greasing the Wheels of Java*.

Peter Delahunty: Delahuntyware . . . . http://blog.peterdelahunty.com
Peter has written several Grails plug-ins and blogs frequently about his experiences, among other things.

James Ervin: Iacobus . . . . http://iacobus.blogspot.com
James is the Groovy Eclipse plug-in project lead and the creator of the Groovy Monkey Eclipse plug-in.

Danno Ferrin: ...And They Shall Know Me by My Speling Errors . . .
. . . http://shemnon.com/speling
Danno is a Groovy committer and a member of the core Griffon development team. He is also a coauthor of the upcoming book *Griffon in Action*.

Robert Fischer: Enfranchised Mind . . . . . . http://enfranchisedmind.com/blog
Robert is the author of *Grails Persistence with GORM and GSQL*, a contributor to GroovyMag, conference speaker, and plug-in author (and all of this while he's working on his divinity degree at Duke—definitely an underachiever!).

Andrew Glover: The Disco Blog . . . . http://thediscoblog.com
Andy is the coolest cat in the Groovy community. He is a frequent conference speaker, coauthor of *Groovy in Action*, and creator of *easyb*, the behavior-driven development framework for the Java platform.

Shawn Hartsock: Thoughts and Ideas . . . . http://hartsock.blogspot.com
Shawn is an enterprise Groovy and Grails expert, Grails plug-in author, and contributor to GroovyMag.

Mike Hugo . . . . http://www.piragua.com
Mike is a Grails plug-in author and contributor to GroovyMag. He has a lot of helpful info on his blog.

Chris Judd: Judd Solutions . . . . http://juddsolutions.blogspot.com
Chris is an author, speaker, trainer, and all-around Groovy guy. He is a coauthor of *Beginning Groovy and Grails: From Novice to Professional*.

Dmitriy Kopylenko: Life Behind Computer Screen...

...http://dima767.github.com

Dmitriy is the creator of GrailCrowd.com and lead author of the online open source *Grails Internals Handbook*.

Ken Kousen: Stuff I've Learned Recently......

...http://kousenit.wordpress.com

Ken is a Java and Groovy trainer, conference speaker, and coauthor of the upcoming book *Making Java Groovy*.

Guillaume Laforge .... http://glaforge.free.fr/weblog

Guillaume is the Groovy project manager, a coauthor of *Groovy in Action*, and a frequent conference speaker.

Tomás Lin: Programming Brain Dump .... http://fbflex.wordpress.com

Tomás is a Grails/Flex expert and author of the online book *Flex on Grails*.

Ted Naleid .... http://naleid.com/blog

Ted is a Grails plug-in author and GroovyMag contributor.

Josh Reed: Josh (formerly) in Antartica...

...http://josh-in-antarctica.blogspot.com

Josh is a desktop Groovy pro and an up-and-coming Griffon power user.

Jim Shingler: Shingler's Thoughts .... http://jshingler.blogspot.com

Jim is a coauthor of *Beginning Groovy and Grails: From Novice to Professional* and a Griffon plug-in author.

Matt Stine .... http://www.mattstine.com

Matt is a Grails plug-in contributor, a Java user group leader, and frequent Groovy/Grails blogger.

Venkat Subramaniam.................... http://www.agiledeveloper.com/blog

Venkat is an internationally recognized speaker and trainer and author of *Programming Groovy: Dynamic Productivity for the Java Developer*.

Matthew Taylor: Dangertree Techblog .... http://weblog.dangertree.net

Matt is a Grails plug-in author extraordinaire and the creator of the Grails plug-in portal. Along with the interesting and informative articles on his blog, he has created some cool screencasts on using the GrailsUI plug-in.

James Williams .... http://jameswilliams.be

James is a Grails committer and member of the core Griffon development team.

Yours Truly: Kickin' Down the Cobblestones...

...http://dave-klein.blogspot.com

You can also reach me at daveklein@usa.net or on Twitter at http://twitter.com/daveklein.

B.3 Other Resources

Besides blogs, websites, and mailing lists, there are many other resources available to new Grails developers. There are books, magazines, podcasts, screencasts, and training organizations.

Books

The shelves are filling up with Groovy and Grails books these days (well, at least mine are). Here's some of the more recent titles.

Grails in Action, **by Glen Smith and Peter Ledbrook**. . .

. . . http://manning.com/gsmith

The Definitive Guide to Grails, **Second Edition, by Graeme Rocher and Jeff Brown**. . .

. . . http://www.apress.com/book/view/1590599950

Programming Groovy, **by Venkat Subramaniam**. . .

. . . http://www.pragprog.com/titles/vslg

Groovy Recipes, **by Scott Davis** . . . . http://www.pragprog.com/titles/sdgrvr

Beginning Groovy and Grails, **by Judd, Shingler and Nusairat**. . .

. . . http://www.apress.com/book/view/9781430210450

Grails Persistence, **by Robert Fischer**. . .

. . . http://www.apress.com/book/view/1430219262

Groovy and Grails Recipes, **by Bashar Abdul Jawad**. . .

. . . http://www.apress.com/book/view/143021600x

Groovy in Action, **Second Edition, by Köenig, King, Laforge and Skeet**. . .

. . . http://www.manning.com/koenig2

Griffon in Action, **by Almiray, Ferrin and Wielenga**. . .

. . . http://www.manning.com/almiray

Other Media

GroovyMag . . . . http://groovymag.com
A monthly e-magazine devoted to Groovy, Grails and Griffon.

The Grails Podcast . . . . http://grailspodcast.com
Sven Haiges and Glen Smith host a biweekly (or as they say, fortnightly) pod-
cast with news, interviews, and interesting discussions centered around the G3
community and technology.

Grails Screencasts . . . . http://www.grails.org/Grails+Screencasts
Grails.org hosts a growing collection of screencasts on topics ranging from Ajax
to JMX to the Grails Mail plug-in.

Training

Even with all of these resources at our disposal, there are times when
having an experienced instructor there to help you dig in can make a big
difference. Don't worry; you're covered there as well. Here are training
opportunities offered by some of the brightest minds in the business.

SpringSource Training http://www.springsource.com/training/grv001

ThirstyHead . . . . http://thirstyhead.com/

GroovyMag Online Training . . . . http://www.groovymag.com/training

Groovy Code Camps . . . . http://www.groovycodecamp.com/

B.4 IDE Support

As I mentioned in Section 2.3, *Setting Up Our Workspace*, on page 22,
many Grails developers find that they don't need an integrated development environment (IDE) as much as they did when working with Java
or other "high-ceremony" languages. In fact, an IDE sometimes gets in
the way. A good text editor, a good browser, and the command line are
often all you need to be productive with Grails. Personally, I use Text-
Mate. My co-worker, who happens to be the best programmer in the
world, uses vi.

That's not to say that there isn't support in the major IDEs. It's just to
let you know that you may not need it once you get going. The three

major Java IDEs—Eclipse, NetBeans, and IntelliJ IDEA—all have vary-
ing degrees of support for Groovy and Grails. NetBeans and IDEA seem
to leapfrog each other as the top G3 IDE, but SpringSource is actively
working on Eclipse's support, so by the time you read this, they may
have leapt to the front. Here are links to information on the support in
each IDE.

Eclipse

Grails Eclipse integration . . . . http://www.grails.org/Eclipse+IDE+Integration

Groovy Eclipse plug-in . . . . http://groovy.codehaus.org/Eclipse+Plugin

Groovy Eclipse on Twitter . . . . http://twitter.com/groovyeclipse

NetBeans

Grails NetBeans integration . . . . http://www.grails.org/NetBeans+Integration

Groovy NetBeans integration . . . . http://groovy.codehaus.org/NetBeans+Plugin

A helpful blog post by Geertjan Wielenga . . .
. . . http://blogs.sun.com/geertjan/entry/running_groovy_on_the_netbeans

IntelliJ IDEA

Grails IDEA integration . . . . http://www.grails.org/IDE+Integration

Groovy IDEA integration . . .
. . . http://groovy.codehaus.org/IntelliJ+IDEA+Plugin+(JetBrains+Edition)

JetBrains Official Groovy/Grails page . . .
. . . http://www.jetbrains.com/idea/features/groovy_grails.html

Appendix C

Bibliography

[Dav08]   Scott Davis. *Groovy Recipes: Greasing the Wheels of Java*. The Pragmatic Programmers, LLC, Raleigh, NC, and Dallas, TX, 2008.

[HT00]   Andrew Hunt and David Thomas. *The Pragmatic Programmer: From Journeyman to Master*. Addison-Wesley, Reading, MA, 2000.

[Koe07]   Dierk Koenig. *Groovy In Action*. Manning Publications Co., Greenwich, CT, 2007.

[Sub08]   Venkat Subramaniam. *Programming Groovy: Dynamic Productivity for the Java Developer*. The Pragmatic Programmers, LLC, Raleigh, NC, and Dallas, TX, 2008.

Index

The Pragmatic Bookshelf

Available in paperback and DRM-free PDF, our titles are here to help you stay on top of your game. The following are in print as of September 2009; be sure to check our website at pragprog.com for newer titles.

Title	Year	ISBN	Pages
Advanced Rails Recipes: 84 New Ways to Build Stunning Rails Apps	2008	9780978739225	464
Agile Coaching	2009	9781934356432	250
Agile Retrospectives: Making Good Teams Great	2006	9780977616640	200
Agile Web Development with Rails, Third Edition	2009	9781934356166	784
Augmented Reality: A Practical Guide	2008	9781934356036	328
Behind Closed Doors: Secrets of Great Management	2005	9780976694021	192
Best of Ruby Quiz	2006	9780976694076	304
Core Animation for Mac OS X and the iPhone: Creating Compelling Dynamic User Interfaces	2008	9781934356104	200
Data Crunching: Solve Everyday Problems using Java, Python, and More	2005	9780974514079	208
Deploying Rails Applications: A Step-by-Step Guide	2008	9780978739201	280
Design Accessible Web Sites: 36 Keys to Creating Content for All Audiences and Platforms	2007	9781934356029	336
Desktop GIS: Mapping the Planet with Open Source Tools	2008	9781934356067	368
Developing Facebook Platform Applications with Rails	2008	9781934356128	200
Enterprise Integration with Ruby	2006	9780976694069	360
Enterprise Recipes with Ruby and Rails	2008	9781934356234	416
Everyday Scripting with Ruby: for Teams, Testers, and You	2007	9780977616619	320
FXRuby: Create Lean and Mean GUIs with Ruby	2008	9781934356074	240
From Java To Ruby: Things Every Manager Should Know	2006	9780976694090	160
GIS for Web Developers: Adding Where to Your Web Applications	2007	9780974514093	275
Google Maps API, V2: Adding Where to Your Applications	2006	PDF-Only	83
Groovy Recipes: Greasing the Wheels of Java	2008	9780978739294	264
Hello, Android: Introducing Google's Mobile Development Platform	2008	9781934356173	200
Interface Oriented Design	2006	9780976694052	240
Land the Tech Job You Love	2009	9781934356265	280

Continued on next page

Title	Year	ISBN	Pages
Learn to Program, 2nd Edition	2009	9781934356364	230
Manage It! Your Guide to Modern Pragmatic Project Management	2007	9780978739249	360
Manage Your Project Portfolio: Increase Your Capacity and Finish More Projects	2009	9781934356296	200
Mastering Dojo: JavaScript and Ajax Tools for Great Web Experiences	2008	9781934356111	568
Modular Java: Creating Flexible Applications with OSGi and Spring	2009	9781934356401	260
No Fluff Just Stuff 2006 Anthology	2006	9780977616664	240
No Fluff Just Stuff 2007 Anthology	2007	9780978739287	320
Practical Programming: An Introduction to Computer Science Using Python	2009	9781934356272	350
Practices of an Agile Developer	2006	9780974514086	208
Pragmatic Project Automation: How to Build, Deploy, and Monitor Java Applications	2004	9780974514031	176
Pragmatic Thinking and Learning: Refactor Your Wetware	2008	9781934356050	288
Pragmatic Unit Testing in C# with NUnit	2007	9780977616671	176
Pragmatic Unit Testing in Java with JUnit	2003	9780974514017	160
Pragmatic Version Control Using Git	2008	9781934356159	200
Pragmatic Version Control using CVS	2003	9780974514000	176
Pragmatic Version Control using Subversion	2006	9780977616657	248
Programming Clojure	2009	9781934356333	304
Programming Cocoa with Ruby: Create Compelling Mac Apps Using RubyCocoa	2009	9781934356197	300
Programming Erlang: Software for a Concurrent World	2007	9781934356005	536
Programming Groovy: Dynamic Productivity for the Java Developer	2008	9781934356098	320
Programming Ruby: The Pragmatic Programmers' Guide, Second Edition	2004	9780974514055	864
Programming Ruby 1.9: The Pragmatic Programmers' Guide	2009	9781934356081	960
Programming Scala: Tackle Multi-Core Complexity on the Java Virtual Machine	2009	9781934356319	250
Prototype and script.aculo.us: You Never Knew JavaScript Could Do This!	2007	9781934356012	448
Rails Recipes	2006	9780977616602	350
Rails for .NET Developers	2008	9781934356203	300
Rails for Java Developers	2007	9780977616695	336
Rails for PHP Developers	2008	9781934356043	432
Rapid GUI Development with QtRuby	2005	PDF-Only	83

Continued on next page

Title	Year	ISBN	Pages
Release It! Design and Deploy Production-Ready Software	2007	9780978739218	368
Scripted GUI Testing with Ruby	2008	9781934356180	192
Ship it! A Practical Guide to Successful Software Projects	2005	9780974514048	224
Stripes ...and Java Web Development Is Fun Again	2008	9781934356210	375
TextMate: Power Editing for the Mac	2007	9780978739232	208
The Definitive ANTLR Reference: Building Domain-Specific Languages	2007	9780978739256	384
The Passionate Programmer: Creating a Remarkable Career in Software Development	2009	9781934356340	200
The Seed of Hope	2009	9781934356357	280
ThoughtWorks Anthology	2008	9781934356142	240
Ubuntu Kung Fu: Tips, Tricks, Hints, and Hacks	2008	9781934356227	400

More Fun with Groovy

Programming Groovy

Programming Groovy will help you learn the necessary fundamentals of programming in Groovy. You'll see how to use Groovy to do advanced programming techniques, including meta programming, builders, unit testing with mock objects, processing XML, working with databases and creating your own domain-specific languages (DSLs).

Programming Groovy: Dynamic Productivity for the Java Developer
Venkat Subramaniam
(320 pages) ISBN: 978-1-9343560-9-8. $34.95
http://pragprog.com/titles/vslg

Groovy Recipes

See how to speed up nearly every aspect of the development process using *Groovy Recipes*. Groovy makes mundane file management tasks like copying and renaming files trivial. Reading and writing XML has never been easier with XmlParsers and XmlBuilders. Breathe new life into arrays, maps, and lists with a number of convenience methods. Learn all about Grails, and go beyond HTML into the world of Web Services: REST, JSON, Atom, Podcasting, and much, much more.

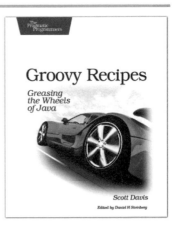

Groovy Recipes: Greasing the Wheels of Java
Scott Davis
(264 pages) ISBN: 978-0-9787392-9-4. $34.95
http://pragprog.com/titles/sdgrvr

Git Yourself Better Tools

Pragmatic Git

There's a change in the air. High-profile projects
such as the Linux Kernel, Mozilla, Gnome, and
Ruby on Rails are now using Distributed Version
Control Systems (DVCS) instead of the old
stand-bys of CVS or Subversion. This book will get
you started using Git in this new distributed world.

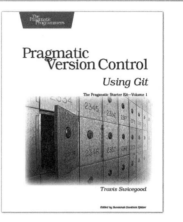

Pragmatic Version Control Using Git
Travis Swicegood
(200 pages) ISBN: 978-1-934356-15-9. $34.95
http://pragprog.com/titles/tsgit

The Definitive ANTLR Reference

This book is the essential reference guide to ANTLR
v3, the most powerful, easy-to-use parser generator
built to date. Learn all about its amazing new LL(*)
parsing technology, tree construction facilities,
StringTemplate code generation template engine,
and sophisticated ANTLRWorks GUI development
environment. Learn to use ANTLR directly from its
author!

**The Definitive ANTLR Reference: Building
Domain-Specific Languages**
Terence Parr
(384 pages) ISBN: 0-9787392-5-6. $36.95
http://pragprog.com/titles/tpantlr

Debug Your Career

The Passionate Programmer

This book is about creating a remarkable career in software development. Remarkable careers don't come by chance. They require thought, intention, action, and a willingness to change course when you've made mistakes. Most of us have been stumbling around letting our careers take us where they may. It's time to take control.

This revised and updated second edition lays out a strategy for planning and creating a radically successful life in software development *(the first edition was released as My Job Went to India: 52 Ways To Save Your Job)*.

The Passionate Programmer: Creating a Remarkable Career in Software Development
Chad Fowler
(200 pages) ISBN: 978-1934356-34-0. $23.95
http://pragprog.com/titles/cfcar2

Land the Tech Job You Love

You've got the technical chops—the skills to get a great job doing what you love. Now it's time to get down to the business of planning your job search, focusing your time and attention on the job leads that matter, and interviewing to wow your boss-to-be.

You'll learn how to find the job you want that fits you and your employer. You'll uncover the hidden jobs that never make it into the classifieds or Monster. You'll start making and maintaining the connections that will drive your future career moves.

You'll land the tech job you love.

Land the Tech Job You Love
Andy Lester
(225 pages) ISBN: 978-1934356-26-5. $23.95
http://pragprog.com/titles/algh

Ready to Deploy?

Release It!

Whether it's in Java, .NET, or Ruby on Rails, getting your application ready to ship is only half the battle. Did you design your system to survive a sudden rush of visitors from Digg or Slashdot? Or an influx of real-world customers from 100 different countries? Are you ready for a world filled with flaky networks, tangled databases, and impatient users?

If you're a developer and don't want to be on call at 3 a.m. for the rest of your life, this book will help.

Release It! Design and Deploy Production-Ready Software
Michael T. Nygard
(368 pages) ISBN: 0-9787392-1-3. $34.95
http://pragprog.com/titles/mnee

Ubuntu Kung Fu

Award-winning Linux author Keir Thomas gets down and dirty with Ubuntu to provide over 300 concise tips that enhance productivity, avoid annoyances, and simply get the most from Ubuntu. You'll find many unique tips here that can't be found anywhere else.

You'll also get a crash course in Ubuntu's flavor of system administration. Whether you're new to Linux or an old hand, you'll find tips to make your day easier.

This is the Linux book for the rest of us.

Ubuntu Kung Fu: Tips, Tricks, Hints, and Hacks
Keir Thomas
(400 pages) ISBN: 978-1-9343562-2-7. $34.95
http://pragprog.com/titles/ktuk

The Pragmatic Bookshelf

The Pragmatic Bookshelf features books written by developers for developers. The titles continue the well-known Pragmatic Programmer style and continue to garner awards and rave reviews. As development gets more and more difficult, the Pragmatic Programmers will be there with more titles and products to help you stay on top of your game.

Visit Us Online

Grails Quick Start's Home Page
http://pragprog.com/dkgrails
Source code from this book, errata, and other resources. Come give us feedback, too!

Register for Updates
http://pragprog.com/updates
Be notified when updates and new books become available.

Join the Community
http://pragprog.com/community
Read our weblogs, join our online discussions, participate in our mailing list, interact with our wiki, and benefit from the experience of other Pragmatic Programmers.

New and Noteworthy
http://pragprog.com/news
Check out the latest pragmatic developments, new titles and other offerings.

Save on the eBook

Save on the eBook versions of this title. Owning the paper version of this book entitles you to purchase the electronic versions at a terrific discount.

PDFs are great for carrying around on your laptop—they are hyperlinked, have color, and are fully searchable. Most titles are also available for the iPhone and iPod touch, Amazon Kindle, and other popular e-book readers.

Buy now at pragprog.com/coupon.

Contact Us

Online Orders:	www.pragprog.com/catalog
Customer Service:	support@pragprog.com
Non-English Versions:	translations@pragprog.com
Pragmatic Teaching:	academic@pragprog.com
Author Proposals:	proposals@pragprog.com
Contact us:	1-800-699-PROG (+1 919 847 3884)